Let Children Come

A Durable Vision
for Christian Schooling

Nicholas Henry Beversluis
Edited by Gertrude Beversluis

C|S **Christian Schools International**
I   Grand Rapids, Michigan

Published by
CHRISTIAN SCHOOLS INTERNATIONAL
3350 East Paris Ave. SE
Grand Rapids, Michigan 49512-3054

© 2001 Gertrude Beversluis
Printed in the United States of America

10 9 8 7 6 5 4 3 2 1

Library of Congress Cataloging-in-Publication Data

Beversluis, N. H. (Nicholas Henry)
   Let children come : a durable vision for Christian schooling / Nicholas
Henry Beversluis ; edited by Gertrude Beversluis — 1st ed.
      p. cm.
   Includes bibliographical references.
   ISBN 0-87463-153-X

   1. Church schools. 2. Christian education. 3. Education—Philosophy.
I. Beversluis, Gertrude. II. Title.

LC368.B48 2001   371.071
                          QBI01-200261

Book design and composition by Joel Beversluis.
Cover layout by Terry Beversluis Glass.

Contents

Acknowledgments

I thank Christian Schools International (CSI) for their willingness to publish this collection of some of Henry's writings. It seems fitting that they should be the ones to do so. During the span of his career in education, Henry served four times on CSI-sponsored committees, addressed quite a few conventions, was published in their journals, and in 1979 made a speaking tour to more than fifty Christian school communities (co-sponsored by Calvin College and CSI). I appreciate, too, the friendliness of CSI staff who worked with me and my family members in finishing up this book.

I thank Dr. Don Oppewal, Professor of Education Emeritus, Calvin College, for his prodding and continued interest in getting this to press. It has greatly encouraged me, Don, that someone in addition to family members believed this project worth doing.

To my son Joel, whose experience in publishing has been a unique aid and who has always been willing to work on this project, from the simplest task of giving computer advice to the intricate one of typesetting and design: thank you, Joel. Thanks also to my daughters: Mary for struggling to transcribe her dad's handwriting and Terry for her contribution to the cover design.

For all my family and friends, and for the life and work of Henry, I thank God.

G. B.

Editor's Preface

What does one do when death takes the loved person who has for years talked optimistically of "getting out a book," and who leaves behind an unpublished doctoral dissertation and boxes of writing ranging from brief notes to five or ten page manuscripts—besides several published booklets and a dozen or so published articles? The resolve to put together a book was inescapable!

That is the story behind this book. It is presented with the hope and prayer which were always Henry's—that his writing would get all sorts of persons to think harder about and to dialogue about the most basic reasons for having Christian schools and the most basic aims such schools should be pursuing. In one note he put it this way, "I hope what I say will be discussion starters for school boards and faculties, for clergymen and consistories, for education department specialists, and for young and old householders in family living rooms."

What is presented in these chapters are Henry's words. Yes, I have had to fill in connecting words and phrases, revise some sentences, rearrange some paragraphs. Since I had typed and critiqued Henry's writing for many years and had much talk with him about ideas and wording, I dared undertake such editing. The epigraphs, except for several from the Bible, are also Henry's words.

However, the choice and arrangement of all materials in this book are mine—and I accept responsibility for whatever extent such choice and arrangement affect the message. In early manuscripts I have changed the word "man" and the personal pronouns, which to Henry at that time were inclusive, to accord with his later practice. Inevitably there are in this book repetitions of key ideas and phrases; I believe they come for the most part with new implications. I trust you, the reader, will be patient with such repetitions, and persistent in exploring the enlarged meanings.

I was concerned to bring to light the work Henry had done in his doctoral dissertation; therefore chapters Four and Ten of this book are excerpts and condensations of parts of that book. Chapters Eleven and Thirteen are earlier published articles; chapter Nine is a complete unpublished manuscript. The remaining chapters I constructed from speech and course notes, a wealth of short and long manuscripts, plus some borrowings from the dissertation and from published materials. Particularly for these chapters I take responsibility for the arrangement and emphasis. My aim is not so much to republish as to preserve Henry's "other ways of saying it."

Fuller discussion of many ideas can be found in his *Christian Philosophy of Education* (especially Chapter 4 regarding goals of education), in *Toward a Theology of Education,* and in other publications; (see *Bibliography*).

Henry's long years in education were a search for what is—or ought to be—distinctive about Reformed Christian education. Immersed as he was in his youth and early teaching years in the problems of those schools which had their beginnings in and were largely supported by the Christian Reformed Church community, it was to them that his thought and writing were first of all addressed. In later years he was convinced that all Christian schools rising from communities which acknowledge the Bible's authority (whether such communities be Lutheran, Roman Catholic, Mennonite, Baptist, or other)—all could and should be based on much the same foundation. In later writings he attempted to address this broader audience. I hope and pray that this collection of his writing will speak to many in that audience. Though the tradition he wrote in and from was the Reformed or Calvinist, and to remain distinctive should be called that, its value for schooling can be appreciated and adopted by parents and educators of many backgrounds.

Henry's experience in education (inspired by teachers he'd had in his late teens) began with an unexpected call, after his discharge from the Navy Chaplaincy, to teach Bible courses at Grand Rapids Christian High School. His year and a half there were a trial (imagine in your first ever teaching facing forty to forty-five high school seniors!) and a challenge. In Henry's words, he found "an anemic religious vision and consequently an anemic educational vision." Nonetheless, he accepted an appointment to teach the same courses at the Eastern Academy (now Eastern Christian High School) in New Jersey. Throughout this time he was dismayed by articles in church and school journals which cited "disarray and drift in Christian education." But at Eastern Academy he found "exciting and productive faculty discussions about the nature and purpose" of such education.

Henry became immersed in work on curriculum and philosophy committees for the eastern schools and for the National Union of Christian Schools (now Christian Schools International, or CSI). He spoke at meetings and conferences, and wrote several journal articles about Christian school bases, aims, and the consequent priority curriculum. He pursued additional graduate study at Union Seminary (New York City) and at Columbia University. All of this led to the lengthy study in his doctoral dissertation which explored the question: "What religious vision must the Christian school begin with?" He wrote, "For schools to claim allegiance to the Bible and the Reformed creeds was hardly a sufficient religious basis for education." He sought a religious vision which could generate educational specifics, which could offer controls on classroom goals, curriculum, and methods.

A phrase prominent in Henry's vocabulary in his later years was taken from a directive of the Christian Reformed Church Synod in 1894, the phrase "reasons of their own." That Synod wanted Christian schooling to be not a branch of the Church, existing mainly to strengthen and propagate the Church, but wanted the schools to be independent of the Church, to be maintained by societies of Christians, and to find and express their own reasons for existence. Uncovering such reasons or bases was the theme of Henry's thought and writing from his time as teacher and principal in New Jersey, in his years as Professor of Education at Calvin

College (Grand Rapids, Michigan), and throughout the years of his retirement. I trust this book will give evidence of his search and conclusions, and pray that it, along with his other published writing, will contribute to the kind of thinking and commitment which results in good Christian schools.

In years of reading C. S. Lewis' Narnia books to our children, Henry had been drawn to the image of children urged into the stable to find there a golden light. A favorite speech closing in his later years was comparing the Christian school to that stable, urging parents and teachers to "let the children come in further, come up higher." More and more through the years he emphasized that all educational thinking and planning was for the sake of the learner, that the true goal was the restoration and maturation of Christian children. For those reasons I have chosen the title *Let Children Come*. May all our children come into the light and freedom of restoration, through Christ, to the service and worship of God in his kingdom on earth.

Gertrude Beversluis
January 2001

A First Story

In whatever way we may understand the creation of man and woman by God, there was a time when they did not exist and there came a time when they did.

Imagine things there in the beginning. Adam and Eve—in the garden. When they come to themselves, they rub their eyes, they think, they exult. Surprised on every hand by joy, they explore, they test, they taste—and rejoice some more. And when they meet God, however this happens, when they hear his voice, know him at the depths of his being, they are neither afraid or inhibited. God and they are related, are friends.

There is no doubt that God is God—holy, boundless, infinite in his plenitude and majesty, overwhelming in his presence. To the man and the woman, God is as overwhelming and glorious as ten billion stars and a field full of flowers, and at the same time as close and intimate as their own breath.

And God said, "It is done; you are here; it is very good."

And God gave them a three-fold command: to love and worship God in true piety—this the forbidden tree and the probationary command told them; to love and serve each other in true community—this the command to be a family, a society, told them; and to love and serve the earth in stewardship—this the cultural mandate told them.

And two trees were set in the garden as symbols, one as a warning against pride and death, the other as a promise of life and fulfillment.

PART I

Present, Past, and Past Present

CHAPTER ONE

Author to Reader

Schooling for the young was not an add-on,
invented by people.
Schooling was in the nature of things.
But a certain kind of schooling.
There was an adjective—it was to be
God-centered *schooling.*

This book is about *religious* schooling. It's about schools where parents look for what through the long ages of time intelligent parents have always seen to be first-class education, plus something more—namely that God does matter just because He exists, matters for everything people do. He matters for their children's growth and development as persons of conscience and competence.

Wanting that something more is true for all who maintain Christian schools. Although I write from within the Reformed Calvinist community and about Reformed ideas, the religious/cultural/educational vision presented here can, I believe, be helpful to any community which strives for distinctive religious schooling.

I want to write not only for educators and education students, but for parents and grandparents, school board members, those who make personal and financial commitments—the ordinary householders of any Christian school community.

We professionals have talked about education to each other and maybe to God but not nearly enough to the people. We have not always helped those rare Jakes and Sallys who still worry about remaining (or becoming more) Reformed in our schools. We have not helped the people explain to their neighbors across the back fence, or to the new members of their church, or to board committees who interview teachers how some of the grand slogans of Christian education still have life in them today.

This book is dedicated to teachers and principals as the stage directors in the drama of education and to parents as those with the right to know, to understand, and to freely evaluate what any one is recommending about their children's schooling.

I use the word *drama*—the *drama* of education—to emphasize that of all human associational undertakings, few bring more passion and disagreement (and personal vulnerability and defensiveness) between people than education. Nor is any undertaking more complex and difficult when it comes to sorting out the particular issues in debate. Yet certain rudimentary convictions tie us all together, and these should be clearly stated.

The Presence of the Past

For Reformed persons and their schools, following the Christian way of life comes wrapped in history, packaged in a tradition. This tradition should not be ignored or squandered. We should draw vision and strength and purpose from it—and, above all, update it and fulfill it. Some of that tradition is barnacled and musty, but most of it, I hold, is religiously vital and educationally provocative.

Already in 1848 a church council (in Holland, Michigan) had urged the establishment of Christian schools to be "the cradle for the church." But Christian schooling did not flourish until after 1880 when a new kind of immigrant from The Netherlands promoted the notion of rearing the young in separate schools. What was to become a profound re-conception of education took hold in the years just prior to 1900—the idea that the schools should no longer be controlled and owned by the churches, but should be independent. This profound change represented the views of the great Dutch scholar and statesman Abraham Kuyper. The cultural-philosophical movement he led declared that each major domain of human activity should be accountable directly to God;

that the school, like every other "sphere," should be sovereign in its own right, existing in a reciprocal relation with other spheres but subordinate only to Christ.

In the 1890s, that philosophy led a Synod of the Christian Reformed Church to turn the Christian schools loose and to encourage the formation of school societies organizationally separate from the church. In effect, Synod said to the schools, "Find reasons of your own for your existence." (That was, I believe, the real birth of Calvinist Christian schools!) Of course, in so approving the change of control from the church to non-parochial citizens' associations, the Synod intended the schools to remain not only Christian but distinctly Reformed. Even so, the change sponsored by perceptive educators and church leaders of the time intended to move the schools out into the wide spaces and challenges of God's world. They must find a religious vision suitable to schooling.

Today the religious question in these schools is more acute because a great many Christian schools have large enrollments of non-Reformed youngsters. Perhaps this is a fullness of time for Christian education in which, through a kind of Pentecost, those of us in the Reformed community can be helped to move into the future by being reminded what our roots really were growing toward through all the past decades. School leaders are being forced to ask not only what's Christian but what's Reformed about our schools. They ask it not to put up ethnic or denominational walls, but in order to retain the central core of Reformed Christian education and to offer that core as its best contribution to non-Reformed youngsters. While we are "lengthening the cords" in a wider admissions policy, we must also be "strengthening our stakes"—must be clear on what and who we are. The answers can also be offered to all Christian educators.

The question is not, Is Christian education nice, is it good, private, elite education, but is it essential? Is it, in short, required by biblical teaching and by loyalty to Jesus Christ?

The questions about Christian education are first of all questions about Christian life. In the final analysis, the size of one's educational ideals and goals will depend on the size of one's religion. Is a person's relation to God to be expressed only or mainly in formal modes of religion and in private morality, or also and necessarily in the totality of daily life? Is the religious part of Christian education to be found only or mainly in "spiritual" experiences in distinction from natural and cultural experiences, or is that religious part also to be a complex of interrelated responses which in the child's life begin to articulate a comprehensive life orientation?

One might say that a Christian school exists as a moment of opposition to secularism, which is a way of life that either denies the existence of God or says that if he exists he does not really matter for much. The Christian day school symbolizes the opposite of this. Its very existence declares that God does exist and that therefore he matters for everything: for all of the subjects studied, for the democratic life we train for, for the cultural ideals we seek to perpetuate—for all of truth, goodness and beauty. The Christian school recognizes that *all of life* must be related to divine standards, and *all* must be subjected to the claims of Jesus Christ and the Kingdom of God.

The Christian school is not an appendage of society or an emergency solution to a crisis in public education. Such a school symbolizes what should be the main concern of any society: the bringing together of our faith in God and our daily activity in "stewarding the earth." According to the Reformed world view, it has to do with a Christian life that, on the one hand, avoids pietism joined to a narrowing and hardened theologizing, and, on the other, avoids cultural accommodationism joined to a dimming and diluting theologizing. It is an expression of a positive philosophy of life.

Educational Philosophy

Perhaps, dear reader, you will say, "What! are you talking philosophy of education? Who needs that?" The answer is, "All the people do, that's who."

When parents in living rooms or in conference with a teacher complain about the novels their youngsters study in school or about the school's new method of teaching science, about report cards, about talk of behavior-modification, about ability grouping, or about art instruction, they are, perhaps unwittingly, engaging in educational philosophy. When a school principal says, as I once heard, that not every child needs to learn to read just as not every child needs to learn to play the violin or bake a cherry pie, he was revealing his educational philosophy.* When Christian Schools International (CSI) prepares Bible study materials along the lines of the Revelation-Response series, it has engaged in educational philosophy. When Calvin College requires of all students certain numbers and kinds of required core courses, it has engaged in educational philosophy. When John Holt and Ivan Illich propose that we de-school society and no longer have compulsory education and thereby free youngsters from adult imposed aims and curriculum, they are engaging in educational philosophy. Actually, the conventional ignorance that calls for abandoning *philosophy* of education and just getting on with good *practices* in education is a counsel not even of despair—but of rank nonsense and confusion.

The reality is that anyone who thinks at all seriously about the *why* or *what* of education is by that much an educational philosopher. Anyone—parent, teacher, board member, clergyman, editor— who ever finds himself or herself saying that something should be abandoned, or changed, or improved about schooling and who gives reasons for the proposal is for better or worse doing educational philosophy. When we think and talk about what Christian thing we are essentially trying to do in these schools that make them *Christian* as schools and about how we are to bring that off—that is engaging in philosophy of Christian education.

Thus the question is not *whether* but *how* we go about it. Because philosophy lurks just below the surface of any serious educational proposal, we must be sure to do it consciously, wisely, productively. It must be educationally useful; that is, it must be in the service of nothing else than good educational practices.

---

*Henry Zylstra also reports hearing this claim. See *Testament of Vision, p. 88.*

I know that people have soured on some kinds of theorizing about education: the blue-sky theologizing that does not touch down into educational reality, or the reactionary slogans that seem mainly aimed to prevent change, or the experimentalist slogans that seem dedicated to nothing but change. So I do understand why the words "educational philosophy" do not normally put a bounce to one's blood pressure or a light in one's eye.

Philosophy of education is not the frightening exercise it is often taken to be, certainly not in Christian schooling where at least the beginning is fairly well located. What is philosophy of education, that of Plato, of Dewey, of the local public school, or of a Christian school? Surely the core of education is transmitting to the young the most deeply cherished beliefs of the adult community. This being so, a simple definition of education philosophy is this: *It is the organization of the school's basic faith commitments for the choosing and testing of its educational aims and its educational practices.*

Of course, educational philosophy holds no magic for quick answers or for removing all frustrations, but it can help concerned persons in profoundly important ways. It can help them by ensuring that the right questions are faced, that similar kinds are grouped together, that they are addressed in the best sequence, and that the best possible answers are carefully and diligently sought out. It can help by thus charting the educational domain more clearly, and thereby guiding concerned persons more directly to the main doorways and central corridors of educational thinking. Good educational philosophy is inclusive, not exclusive; it should bring people together, not build walls.

I have sometimes thought of philosophy of education as the *music* of education—the possible beauty, the harmony of ultimate matters. It is talk about the nature of a person, about how people learn, and what they can know. The liberating vision of Christian education, the world view controls upon Christian education, the radically clarifying philosophy—that is the *music.*

The Priority Question

The crucial first question for a Christian philosophy of education will therefore be the nature and scope of biblical religion. Without agreement on that there cannot be agreement on the ways religion ought to affect education. The most important matters to a school will be its religious perspective on the kingdom of God, on history, on society, on culture, on nature—all of them in their inter-relatedness. The school's religious view concerns also the nature of human beings, personal self-acceptance, religious growth, and calling in life.

Persons holding a restricted view of religion will answer these questions in far different ways than persons who hold a comprehensive view of religion. Some writers warn about fundamentalist tendencies in the schools which, they say, lead to sociological segregation, cultural withdrawal, and religious irrelevance. Others warn about liberal religious tendencies in education which, they say, lead to worldliness, loss of distinctiveness, cultural assimilation, and a denial of the antithesis between Christianity and unbelief. To find common ground and to be convinced of the need for Christian day schools, we must get clear on biblical teaching about what Christians must be and do in the world, about Christ and culture, about worldly holiness.

The organizing of our faith commitments—yes, for the sake of the child! Teachers, principals, and parents must understand and respect child-life and adolescent-life—as the life of those of whom the Lord said, Let them come to me. To enhance our knowledge about these learners we need scientific and psychological data, but above all we need biblical, revelational data, both descriptive and prescriptive.

What must the image-of-God child be and do? What needs for religious growth must the school reckon with? Adam's children, the Psalmists' children, your neighbor's children, your children, all Christian children—what needs do these all have in common, if religion is to involve all of life, all the time? Here again, to know children's important needs and to be effective Christian schools, we must search out and agree on a *biblical* religious vision.

21

This is not to ask for a uniformity and consensus that curb experiment and openness to new challenges and opportunities. Christian school education must never become frozen or doctrinaire; it must be open to new understandings about the child and the learning process, to new techniques for teaching, and to the new demands of modern life. As creativity must become permanent in the student's life so must it in the lives of teachers, principals, and school boards. However, consensus on certain basic matters not only is compatible with openness and creativity but is indispensable to them. Only when what is known, believed, and firmly fixed are generally agreed on as common premises will Christian educators be freed for discussion, experimentation, and diversity in practices. Then the diversity will be neither threatening nor unhealthy; rather, the climate for a both conservative and progressive Christian education will have been created.

The basic religious questions and vision are a perennial concern. Because the answers are subtle, they need attention over and over again. My aim is to seek a way in which two things may come more clearly into view: a religious perspective which is more educationally significant and an educational enterprise which in turn will be more religiously significant. I believe the concepts I develop in this book may reasonably be invoked as guides and controls for an education that by definition seeks to be biblical in its scope and thrust.

CHAPTER TWO

A Durable Tradition

*Into the primitive forest of western Michigan
came a uniquely sophisticated theory
of school government
and a sort of Augustinian notion of culture-and-religion.*

In their more than one hundred year history, the Calvinist Christian schools have existed, as indicated in Chapter One, within a tradition. This Reformed tradition has valued a way of thinking and a way of living; a way of interpreting history and a way of reading the Bible; and a way of accepting the Christian's vocation in the world under the real and present lordship of Jesus Christ. By *Reformed* is meant a way of understanding and obeying God's three great commands, which were given in the beginning in the garden and reaffirmed through Christ's restoration of "all things." These are the commands to love God above all, in personal piety; to love one another in human community; and, under the impulse and power of those loves, to do the world's work in cultural affirmation and transformation.

In Reformed thinking a theology and a world and life view complement the *biblical* perspective that religion is both a personal relationship and a comprehensive life orientation. The theological tradition combines the intellectual vigor of Calvin with his "religion of the burning heart." It follows Calvin's emphasis on the covenantal themes of God's sovereignty and grace, human creaturehood and sinfulness, human calling to stewardship before the face of God, and moral accountability in the totality of life. On the one hand, a cherished doctrinal summary, the Heidelberg Catechism, speaks in vital religious language of both human experience and divine-human relationships. On the other, the tradition of a world and life view, supporting the perspective of religion as comprehensive, warns against the dualism of separating nature from grace. It speaks of the claims of Christ in all spheres of life, and emphasizes the cultural mandate of Genesis. Writers in this tradition agree that religion must be expressed in the totality of life.

In addition, a confidence has come down to us, and a Reformed instinct, itself enlarged in the stream of western Christian civilization. Back beyond Reformed leaders of the recent centuries, back in John Calvin, in Augustine, in St. Paul, we discover this affirmation: born for eternity, a pilgrim on the earth, at cross purposes here, there, and always with persons of ill-will, of indifference, of darkness, Christian believers have here still a life to live, a judgment to announce, a gospel to tell, a claim to stake, a garden to dress. Human destiny in Christ is envisaged in two phases: to be restored and thereupon to be matured. As persons and as the elect community we are to be restored by divine grace, to this end: to know God, to enjoy Him and to glorify Him increasingly here and now.

From these traditions we learn that the purpose of religion surely is not just to give human beings a pep talk as they stumble through the shadowlands of history. Religion is *big* in the sense that its purpose is infinitely more than the negative one of saving us from despair and punishment and eternal death. It is big because it aims at nothing less than our re-establishment in covenant fellowship with God, so that our minds are freed to know the truth, our wills are freed to do the right, and our hearts are freed for love and beauty.

Diminished Christianity

Indeed one of the crises of our age is the acceptance of a shrunken Christianity. It seems at times that some custodians of the gospel have decided upon a frantic eleventh hour attempt to market Christianity at any price, so long as it is kept small and simple, so long as it provides pat solutions, and is not costly, and does not

24

challenge us in our self-centeredness. They persuade people that peace of mind is most important and can easily be obtained, or that escape from a future punishment is all that matters now, and that this can be achieved by momentary religious experience. Above all they try to establish not that humankind exists for God, but that God exists for us. The result is a kind of pseudo-religious psychology: we are told that Christian faith will win us friends and influence God, and will turn all anxiety and tension into contentment and peace of mind.

More serious is the stunting of religion among some of the gospel's evangelical adherents. The "dear Jesus" religion of our day, in proclamation and in songs, is in danger of reducing a genuine experience of the living Christ to formulas, to clichés, to words and slogans. Though these words may be used genuinely and in sincere faith, they are often misused, or even profanely used. Often the words are substituted for the facts, the repetition for the experience, the sound for the substance; the glorious gospel is inverted into a kind of sentimental selfishness.

If all this is not a distortion of the gospel, it is a reducing of it, making it thin and emaciated. There is little of its scope and covenantal quality left. Such a religion is quite foreign to the Hebrew-Christian origins of Christianity—unknown, say, to Moses and Isaiah, John the Baptist and St. Paul. The saints and martyrs and reformers of old-fashioned Christianity gloried rather in the visions and tensions of a big and costly and God-centered faith. The true human need is to be restored to all the fullness of manhood and womanhood, into a covenant life with God. Had Adam in the Garden asked, What is the chief end of humanity? surely the answer would have been: to know God, to enjoy and to glorify God forever. This is still the answer of the Bible and of the saints of all times. This is the Reformed tradition.

The Tradition and Education

Within this tradition many of us have been saying for about a hundred years now that Christian education is the cornerstone of a Reformed way of life and that for this reason it must increasingly become more Christian and better education. This has meant, more or less plainly, that people have been concerned through their schools to provide the best of formal, liberal arts education, under the light and discipline of the Bible. The schooling was to reach and form the whole person, the real person, the human person, the person defined as image bearer of God.

Can school communities make progress in defining this mission? To do so we must distinguish between *Reformed* as a set of church creeds and *Reformed* as a world view, a way of understanding, of choosing, and of acting in the world as God's people. We must examine our times and the tradition for new language or fit the old language with new and enriched content. And above all, the language (e.g., glory of God, kingdom, discipleship, and the like) must meet the test of classroom relevance. If it does not, we should discard it or re-focus it. In stating a Reformed vision for schooling, it is not enough to say the good or true things that any organization could say, whether Sunday Schools, youth fellowships, mission stations, or fundamentalist school associations. We must try to say *distinctive* things, that startle people, intrigue them, and become challenges to yes or no responses. We should avoid code words and labels that short-circuit or become substitutes for serious thinking.

Almost as important for Reformed evangelicals as the question of biblical infallibility is this question of what sort of religious life the Bible calls us to. Disagreement exists on both questions, but most of us get much more excited about the infallibility question than the religious question. I think this is wrong. Leaving the religious question unfaced or unresolved makes it look like our concern about the Bible is only doctrinal or theoretical. It also makes it look as though those evangelicals with a narrow view of religious calling speak for all of us. Further, without a mature and vigorous answer to the question about the appropriate religious life we continue to look like a forty million member sect in America, living off this or that ecclesiastical parent.

Most significantly, without a view of religious calling commensurate with the beauty and majesty of the Holy Bible, we have

26

no adequate basis for Christian elementary and secondary day school education—nor for that matter for Christian higher education. I am saying not that evangelicals need Christian schools more than anything else but that we need a deep and wide religion more than anything else. But then I add this: that such a big religious vision will both require and produce Christian schools.

What is the "Big" Religious Vision?

A big religious vision means that worship gets bred in the bone. Where practicing the presence of God nourishes prayer. Where sin in its darkness and ugliness are not covered over with happy Jesus talk. Where prayer has the mood of David's prayer, "against thee, thee only have I sinned;" or the publican's, of Jesus' parable, "Lord have mercy." Where prayer is followed by the assurance that nothing can separate us from the love of God, neither height nor depth nor things present nor things to come—nothing. And it means the Psalms and the great hymns of the church are sung, and not just frothy, titillating gospel ditties. A big religion means being at home in the Psalms, sensing the majesty of Isaiah, understanding a bit of why even Jesus went apart to pray. It means that anything in the school chapel that comes after singing "My God how wonderful thou art" is anticlimax.

Second, a big religion also means, in our worship of God, looking outward to fellow human beings as God's image bearers, not asking callously, "Am I my brother's keeper?" It means knowing what Jesus meant by the parable of the Good Samaritan; understanding both Moses and Jesus when they said the second commandment is to love your neighbor as yourself. It means to understand why everywhere from Moses, through the prophets, and in Jesus' teaching, we read about the poor, the stranger, the widow and orphan, the sick, the weary, the hungry, the dispossessed—how not only sin and punishment are described in terms of our response to such, but also obedience and blessedness.

Third, a big religion means looking outward too at this world, God's creation, as the area in which we are to love God and our neighbor. It means understanding that all creation is the Lord's, as

Psalm 24 says, and that we his image bearers are still crowned with glory and honor to have sovereignty over all things. It means that we should do the world's work: in day labor, in offices, in factories, in science and art, in poetry and music. We must celebrate the wonders and mysteries of the creation, God's goodness and guidance in civilization and history, by adding to the splendid works of others. Our faith must be enriched and fulfilled in an extensive religious response that thrusts us into the fullness of human life; work and worship are to be a seamless whole. This is the tradition in which we live. This the Christian schools need to proclaim, practice, and test themselves against.

But then it must be emphasized that doctrines bearing directly on educational aims and practices ought not to be muted or compromised. There is a necessary, even indispensable, depth and range of theology that good Reformed Christian education is rooted in and nourished by. Its rudiments are: a commitment to the Bible in its totality, to biblical theology as a way of reading the Bible, and to the unity of God's covenant in two testaments; a commitment to the covenant as relationship between God and persons, having to do with not only "spiritual" life but with our natural, daily existence; a commitment to Christ as mediator, through whom "all things" were created and were restored, and as Lord—lord in not just a future but a present kingship, in not merely our private lives but in a public kingship requiring transformation of the structures and institutions of our society; and a commitment therefore to both personal and cultural obedience in our lives as adults and in our rearing of the young.

If we have been saying some of these things for a hundred or so years, the danger exists that they have in some part become clichés. Where slogans replace meaning, and combinations of words replace meanings in conflict, the gates are open to subversion or to sentimentality. So it has been politically and religiously down the ages into our own time.

If we would avoid this, or overcome it, and if we would remain vigorous, we shall have to push ourselves, in our generation, through the underbrush and up the hills of fervent thought and discussion, as those before us did. We shall neither understand nor advance beyond them if we do not, like them, experience the sweat and toil of mind meeting mind, of yielding up prejudices, of ourselves climbing the slopes. We shall either imagine we have reached the upland country or remain resigned—or content—in the bottomlands of Reformed life and thought. In that event we shall be less than able to maintain our faith against its modern detractors and opponents. Let no one be indifferent or say that this is much ado about nothing. There is a sense in which a community's philosophy of education is no more nor less than its philosophy of life, its world and life view. We live within a durable tradition; it is our part to mold and enrich it for our times.

CHAPTER THREE

So, What's a Good Christian School?

One way to discuss Christian schools is to try to get at the idea of them, the positive reason for having them, the fringe and the core benefits they offer young Christians in the classrooms.

In each generation, decisions must be made by parents about the schooling of their children. As they consider their local Christian school, they ask: Are Christian schools worth their formidable cost? One cost is time and work, the cost to school boards and committees. For parents, current tuition costs could be asking cruel and unusual stewardship of the average householder. Another cost is to the child. Denying young Christians the social and psychological benefits, as well as the moral challenges, of a shared school life with their neighborhood friends risks a deprivation and an alienation that could adversely affect their common citizenship later in life. A fourth cost is to the public schools. To withhold from the public schools many thousands of young persons reared in stable and God-fearing homes seems to be, especially in these days of tumult in the public schools, if not wicked, then certainly un-American. Only a *good* Christian school, one that positively and creatively presents the whole range of the Christian way of life, can justify such costs to parents, to children, and to the public schools.

A good Christian school is not first of all a kind of institutional shield against drugs, sex, and profanity—or against questionable novels or ideas such as evolution. It is also not a week-day church concerned mainly with child evangelism. It is not a surrogate home-away-from-home, releasing parents from their obligations to nurture children in the rudimentary knowledge and practices of godliness. A good Christian school does not reject secular humanism at the front door and then admit the jingoism and lifestyle of American civil religion at the back door. It obviously is not a device for dodging bussing or integration laws or, more subtly, a device for discriminating against poor or disadvantaged children by refusing to adjust for them its tuition charges or educational methods. And a good Christian school does not subvert education by tolerating inferior facilities, teachers, or academic standards as long as devotional periods are regularly held, Bible studies are in place, or "worldly" subjects are screened, cleaned, and baptized with cautionary homilies. A good Christian school will warn against evil with it many faces, but will not be narrow or subversive in such ways.

A good Christian school is a school with a big religious vision, a comprehensive life orientation, where academic excellence, first-rate pedagogy, and Christianity enrich each other and together shape that religious vision. It is a school where a chief concern of the teachers is to transmit to young Christians that vision and its significance for daily living. A Christian school is good when its teachers are clear in their own heads and hearts about what Christians must be and do in the world, clear about Christ and culture, and about worldly holiness; and when their teaching reflects that understanding. Such teachers are persuaded that Christianity is in fact so wide-ranging and all-encompassing that although it joyfully celebrates and promotes personal faith and godliness, its work-a-day religiousness goes far beyond the personal in what we have long called a world-and-life view. Almost the whole case for Christian schools depends on teachers having this religious vision and teaching it, wisely, developmentally, and pedagogically to the young. Such a school gives young persons, as Dr. Henry Zylstra of Calvin College said many years ago, "more to be Christian with."[*]

---

[*] Dr. Zylstra, Professor of English, wrote and spoke significantly about Christian education in the mid-20th century.

Christian education should be big in the way St. Paul must have understood it when he exclaimed in amazement about the depth of the riches both of the wisdom and knowledge of God (Rom.11). Or when he declared that the God's truth, God's grace, were given not only to make us wise unto salvation *from* something, but also to make us complete persons, sons and daughters, men and women wholly equipped for right living. Christian education must be big in the way the Psalms present it: the earth and its fullness are the Lord's (Ps. 24) and human persons, created but little lower than God, are crowned with glory and honor for religious stewardship in the earth (Ps. 8).

In the biblical perspective, religious response to God's glory and goodness is not to be a kind of beatific vision that lifts us up and out of every day to a spiritual realm above ordinary life. Rather, it is to be a response from within the fullness of our daily life, thrusting us out into all of the natural, societal, and cultural conditions of our existence. According to the Bible, we are to affirm the world and do the world's work, all intertwined with our worship of God.

Religion was big, that way, in the beginning in the garden, before the fall, and is so in the restoration of all things through Christ. Through Christ our vocation to do the world's work is renewed, and doing that work to the praise of God is again possible. Let us say it again, as did the Dutch theologian Herman Bavinck: the Christian needs two conversions, one away from the world to Jesus Christ, the other in the name of Christ back to the world. Christianity in the perspective of both creation and redemption is a big religion, aiming also at that second conversion. Parents and a community who believe children must grow in such religion need Christian schools to help them.

Such a big religious vision, carefully communicated to young persons in school, should impel them outward into life and the world as their proper domain. It should direct them outward into the realities of nature and society, culture and history, as religious vocation. They must learn to accept each day as a gift for celebrating ordinary life in the world. Such *whole* religion must help young persons in the schools to accept life's common problems and complexities, its tensions and obligations, its opportunities and challenges as part of their being called religiously in and to the world. In Christian schools, young persons must learn worldly obedience and also celebration, because they hold a native citizenship in the world.

If in a Christian school young persons grow in understanding and accepting such native citizenship, they will be changed, matured, religiously. They will grow toward accepting a shared life with their neighbors in ordinary societal relationships. They will learn that such a shared life means being burdened, religiously as Christians, with the common burdens—with political corruption, with sexual permissiveness, with ghetto unemployment, with gun and vehicle violence—and also with the common opportunities—with writing novels, with cures for cancer, with good architecture, and all the rest. Such native citizenship means they will be caught up in the these concerns as part of their worship of God and their obedience to him.

Of course, such education for worldly obedience brings great risks. Young Christians need to learn that religious response within the world means not accommodating themselves to or being seduced by evil; it means not forgetting that the assumptions and values of contemporary society are in many ways demonic; and not forgetting that even saints can fall away. But religious life in the world means too that they must plant their trees and light their candles. Such response means that although they are pilgrims seeking the eternal city, they must learn to live as God's men and women in humanity's common society and common history until our Lord returns; they must learn that under the sign of that double citizenship, Christians have no choice but to affirm the world. Compelled by a big religious vision to accept both the risk and the promise, good Christian teachers and principals know their job. In their schools, young Christians mature to become the complete persons for whom God's redemptive word and acts were given.

Aiming at such education, a good Christian school is not a negative phenomenon. It is not an emergency solution to this or that crisis in public schools. It is not a fringe movement or a sectarian aberration in society. A good Christian school does not educate for a Christian ghetto existence outside the American mainstream. It does not foster inferiority or superiority complexes in students or teachers. Rather, in the best tradition of both schooling and Christianity, it is positive and constructive. It is *affirmational*. It comes up out of, and in turn gives expression to, a big religious vision, somewhat as described in the foregoing. It is a school where, as Henry Zylstra said, nothing human is alien, where we are involved up to the hilt in life.*

Such a school rejects not only the secularism that denies God's existence, but also the kind that worships him only in a realm *above* ordinary life, in holy places and in holy acts apart from the concreteness of every day. A Christian school affirms by its existence and in its educational program that God does exist and matters for everything, especially for everything any good school is busy with: the subjects studied, the democratic life we prepare for, the cultural ideals we seek to perpetuate. In such a school young Christians are guided and prodded to live an examined life, a life examined under the light and discipline of the Bible.

Therefore, whether in fourth grade or in eleventh grade, a well-taught curriculum should prod young persons to enlarge and reconstruct their familiar world and induct them into the world they ought to know. The curriculum should compel them, for example, to see the poverty in their city that they never saw before—to understand it, to probe its causes, and to be concerned about its cures. The curriculum should bring them to ask about happenings and causes in the physical world they never before asked or thought about; to hear things in music and see things in art they never heard or saw before; to live vicariously into the mysteries and complexities of human existence as these are probed in myth and drama and novels.

---

* *Testament of Vision*, p. 133

A school curriculum is of supreme importance; it is a gift of common and uncommon grace, to believer and unbeliever alike. The Christian school curriculum must make young persons curious, knowledgeable, concerned about all sorts of things: about the development through the centuries of tools and science as well as poetry and architecture; about the relation between twentieth century wars and twentieth century cynicism; about the history of their country and the history of their church, as well as about modern medicine and modern nationalism. The curriculum should disclose to young persons the tensions of contemporary life and prod them to seek more subtle understandings, to face more difficult choices than they by nature are inclined to seek, and in these ways to become more willing and able participants in that life—in their future but also day by day in their own reconstructed experience.

But then this above all must happen: the teaching must all be focused for *religious* growth, for living the examined life, for testing the spirits, for discrimination, for moral choice, for giving young persons "more to be Christian with." Which is to say that although a Christian school does not exist mainly for provincial or negative reasons, one of its major concerns all along the way is to promote intellectual and moral discrimination. To foster such informed discrimination, Christian teachers have a major obligation to help young persons probe the ideas and allegiances that a good curriculum discloses. Such probing must be directed toward all sorts of issues, ranging from civil disobedience, theories of creation and evolution, and good and bad novels, to modern advertising, human sexuality, labor unions and welfare programs. If not easy answers or pat formulas but the habit of informed discrimination is insisted upon, religious sensitivity and obedience can be quickened and enriched.

Of course, such emphasis on intellectual and moral discrimination in no way requires a kind of geiger-counter approach to subject matter, ruining literature or science or history in a gimlet-eyed search for heresy. The teacher's first concern, a professional and religious obligation, is to teach good subject matter well. Only as part of that obligation comes also the probing for the good and the bad, the true and the false, and—most important for education—the gray areas, the tensions, the ambiguities between right and wrong, good and bad.

This too is true: what good Christian schooling needs, to match all this, is first-rate professional competence. Within the priority subject matter, the right sorts of teaching must go on so that learning takes place. What should characterize Christian education is not the moralizing and repression of young persons, but their enlargement of mind, of commitment, of personal freedom. Through excellent pedagogy and the best help psychology and sociology can give, the teacher should aim at keeping learner and subject matter in range of each other.

Being professional and Christian in these ways is to say that a good Christian school must bring together the proven vitalities of both traditional and modern education, focused for *Christian* education. In such a school, good subject matter and vital learning must make religion more humanly relevant and the human more religiously compelling. If such education happens, the school will be doing that for which it is most needed. It will be integrating academic excellence with the Christian religion in such a way that each enriches the other, and both help young Christians to understand and live the Christian life. Such a school will be giving young persons, all along the way, "more to be Christian with."

PART II

Religious Vision for Christian Schooling

CHAPTER FOUR

The Biblical Foundations

The comprehensiveness of religion is determined in the reality of man's covenantal union with God as it was established in creation and restored through Christ.

*I will put my law within them,
and I will write it upon their hearts;
I will be their God and they shall be my people.*
Jer. 31:33

If Christian education is to be made relevant to modern times and issues, it should be made relevant not by ignoring or abandoning but by grappling with the religious question. Though it is first of all a question of life and faith, it will need to be seen as inherent in the very concept of Christian education. Without agreement on the nature and scope of religion, there cannot be agreement on the ways it ought to affect education, how it ought to determine not only general aims, but also specifics of method and curriculum. It is imperative, therefore, that we search the biblical foundations.

Christian educators have in common a commitment to the Bible's authority, a belief that the Bible is the inspired word of God through and to man, in both Testaments. The approach to the Bible taken here will in the main be that of biblical rather than systematic theology. This means a theology based not in the creeds as such, not in dogmatics as the church's logical organization of Christian truth, but one based in biblical revelation as it developed historically in the self-disclosure of God and in the response to that self-disclosure by human persons in their historical life. The way of biblical theology is the way of seeing redemption in the perspective of creation, of letting the theology of the profoundly important Genesis revelation guide and inform our thinking about all of the God-human relationship set forth in the Bible.

Nature and Scope of Religion

The Bible presents religion as ultimate relationship, as living always "before the face of God." Such religion is ultimate, *first*, with respect to its objective anchorage in God and in all of reality as both encounter persons; and *second*, such religion is ultimate with respect to its subjective anchorage in full human response to that encounter. The first aspect has to do with the range and comprehensiveness of revelation and the second with the depth dimension of personal faith and commitment.

Though all religions represent some kind of relationship, the contemporary emphasis upon ultimacy goes beyond most traditional conceptions to stress both aspects of religion. This approach clarifies the need for not only concreteness but for comprehensiveness as well; it sees religion as the ultimate concern of an individual in all of life, in work and worship, in "worldly" things as well as in the "spiritual." The Bible has all along uniquely emphasized religion in both aspects of ultimacy, both its objective inclusiveness and its subjective passion and commitment.

In the beginning, according to Genesis, the man and the woman were placed in the garden with a task, but also at once confronted with the fact of their accountability to an order and a Being above them. Thus God himself established the conditions of relationship in his creation of the man and woman and in endowing them with his image; he maintained relationship by revealing himself to them. They were to conform to his will and purpose and to respond in worship and work. Biblical religion involves a life of activity, of program, and of concern in the midst of the world, but also a quietness and an expectancy in which persons wait upon God. The key to such religion is that it is a dynamic, ongoing relationship. It is the moving and shaking at the depths of life that comes when a person is laid hold upon by a God who is known and who bids that person walk in his way. It involves the totality of everyday worldly life, for that is the life which must be lived in the presence of God and offered to God.

Biblical Religion Means Covenant

It is in the metaphor of covenant that the Bible sets forth this view of God and human beings in the totality of their inter-relatedness. Covenant is the religious arrangement ordering ultimate relations between God and humanity. There are two foci in this covenant: *first*, the transcendent and holy God created the world and humankind and, by means of self-revelation, entered into personal communion with people; *second*, the conditions in which and through which human beings respond to God's revelation are the realities of nature, of society, and of history. The world of diversity, of contingency, of possibility, is the place where men and women live both freely and responsibly in covenant with God.

In this covenant, God is incomprehensible, holy, righteous, all-powerful, all-knowing, transcendent; but he is also the immanent one: the friend of Abraham, the father who pities his children, the Immanuel. God is at the same time the one who is unapproachable on Mt. Sinai and the one who dwells with his children in the tabernacle. On the other hand, human beings are the finite ones, the creatures, sharing finitely in only some of the divine perfections, altogether dependent, and called upon to offer God worship and adoration; they are also image of God, sons and daughters of God, free, responsible, and caretakers of creation.

Thus, in the biblical perspective, the covenant, though not between equals, is between partners, each of whom binds himself to but also lays claims upon the other. The possibility of this partnership lay in the image of God in human beings. Its means was the Word spoken and received, a Word creative of humanity and creative also of communion. Through the love and obedience which covenant required and the hallowed work which was its purpose, the man and woman would grow in the capacity to worship God and grow in communion with him. This the Reformed creeds express when they speak of "knowing God and enjoying Him."

This covenant relationship is set forth in the Bible in a series of "installments" which form a continuum from creation to the redemptive consummation. The creation covenant is universal and permanent; it gives the man and the woman their special status and assignment (Gen.1:26-28; 2:7-8). In the next step, the alliance against the Serpent, God indicates that he will not let them "die" after their sin; he will take their side against Satan and set up a spiritual antithesis in human history (Gen. 3:15-24). The so-called covenant of nature, after the flood, guarantees the natural conditions for human history; it reaffirms human responsibility and stewardship in nature (Gen. 8:21-22; 9:8-17). The covenant with Abraham inaugurates a concentration of God's grace upon an elect nation during the long history until the birth of Christ (Gen. 17:7). In the national or Sinaitic covenant, the given law—civil, ceremonial, and moral—becomes the way for expression of gratitude and devotion; ceremony and ritual were regarded not as ends but as means to and symbols of the inner reality of religion (Exod. 19:56). The prophets announce the failure and passing of that narrow national covenant and point to a "new covenant" in which the moral law is written in the heart, the outward compulsions of ceremony and place are abolished, and God's favor is extended to all nations and peoples (Jer. 31:31-33). The last age of the covenant, including especially its fulfilled universalism, is inaugurated at the coming of Christ and goes on throughout the Christian era.

Nevertheless, the essence of the internal covenant had been present from the beginning. Joshua says, "Choose this day;" Samuel tells the king, obedience is better than sacrifice; the Psalms declare God's delight in the contrite, loving heart. The prophets remind the people that God has shown what is good (Micah 6:8) and proclaim his promise, "I will be their God, and they shall be my people." And Christ saves from sin so that we may "love God above all, and our neighbor as ourselves." As sin radically enlarged the distance between God and humankind, so grace radically closed the distance, so that, as a result of the sin-grace continuum there is an even greater sense of reverence and worship, on the one hand, and of communion and friendship, on the other.

That idea of covenant is the all-encompassing perspective in which to view the Bible in both of its Testaments. In that perspective of the unity of the covenant, the Bible and the covenant of grace are themselves subordinate within a larger wholeness. Both are seen to relate to an earlier reality, namely, the creation covenant with God, a covenant which though broken by sin is restored through divine redemption. The redemptive covenant cannot be understood in its full religious and educational significance except in relation to the creation covenant. This concept of restoration of the creation order becomes crucial for both religion and education.

Restoration through Christ

We must ask, then, can it be shown on the basis of biblical evidence that Christ's work restores and reaffirms the creation covenant? Can it be shown that everything human and natural participates in the reality and meaning of redemption? Can it be shown that a "born again" person should live a creation life in nature, in society and in culture, as both Christian and natural person? Did Christ restore the Genesis mandate so that it in turn undergirds and helps define the missionary mandate of Matthew 28? I believe the Bible supports this understanding of restoration.

That Christ is Mediator of creation is clearly taught: in John's Gospel, "all things were made through him" (John 1:1-4); in Hebrews, "a Son, through whom he created the world" (Heb. 1:2-3); and in Colossians, "all things were created through him and for him" (Col. 1:16-17). In keeping with this profound investment of himself in creation, Christ became its restorer also. He came not merely to restore individuals to the Father, but to restore society; and not merely society, but divine purpose in nature and history and all of creation as well. He came for the redemption of "all things" from the sin and judgment under which they had fallen—

"through him to reconcile to himself all things, whether on earth or in heaven" (Col.1:19-20). Christ is pre-eminently the reconciler of human persons to God, but that means nothing less than to be restored to covenant, to relationship, to a covenant which includes "all things" as the *conditions* of human religious life.

Thus the salvation of all things, with human beings at the center, relates to creation in two ways: the Logos of creation is also the Logos of reconciliation, and that which was created, the object of creation, is also the object of reconciliation. It is the old made over: the same image of God, the same covenant, the same world, and the same history in which now the life of covenant must again be lived. Only because they are the old can we speak of it as reconciliation: "God was in Christ reconciling the world to himself" (II Cor. 5:17-19).

Beginning in the old sacrifice and fulfilled in the new, humanity's redemption, like its creation, was for the sake of a relationship of life, of communion. For this covenantal goal Christ assumed the redemptive role and became the center of history. Reconciliation and new life were given so that people may become what they could have become; so that community and nature and work may again be put back into the way of God's will; and so that the kingdom of God may give point and purpose to all human activities. Through Christ the old was made new and once again given to humankind: "for all things are yours, and you are Christ's, and Christ is God's" (I Cor. 3:21-23).

In the biblical ideal, the vertical reality of God enters into every earthly reality. It causes the Psalmist to say: Whom have I in heaven besides thee? This is one great theme of the Bible; another is that earth and its fullness are the Lord's. These two together suggest that it is in the conjunction of work and worship that God must be met. Not to meet him there is to violate the covenant. Humankind is reminded to seek God in the diversity, the plenitude, the fullness of this world; that is, they are forbidden to seek only the "way up" to God.

Therefore the creation covenant is not merely a first covenant, but the one that encompasses and gives full significance to the others. This continuity of covenant gives religious meaning to all of creation and to all of history. Without the creation perspective, the meaning of redemption itself is impoverished, and is related to a truncated view of religion and of human obligation and calling. The creation covenant perspective fosters a fuller view of Christ's authority, of religion in the midst of life, of human culture as religious obligation, and of Christian education as the agent of such religion and such culture.

The Two Conditions of Covenant Relationship

According to the Bible, revelation is the central reality of God's interaction with human beings. We by searching do not find out God, but God finds us and reveals himself as he comes to us (Job11:7; Rom.1-3). Without such revelation, systems of truth and morality can neither be comprehensive nor evoke ultimate commitment, because beyond them is always the impersonal and undemanding "unknown God." But by means of revelation through word and act, God gives meaning to all things. The revelation is comprehensive in that the meaning which it brings embraces both the natural order of creation and the trans-natural order of God as creator and as reconciler. Our response to such revelation must be the appropriate one of a concerned search for meanings; it must be response in the ultimate commitments of faith and obedience. As taught in the Bible, religion needs those two conditions of relationship: God's encounter of us through his word and work and human response to God in work and worship.

For us, the central revelation on which all relationship depends is that God created all things and that he loves and saves us (Gen.1:1-2.3; John 3:16). Revelation is presented as more than a message about events; it is first of all the events themselves. The acts of God bring forth our response, as they brought forth both creation and redemption. This revelation is God's giving of himself; it becomes the basis of covenant relationship; it is the word of origin and power.

The Bible shows that this power is supremely true of God's word as *Logos:* creation was by the Word and redemption was by the Word—the same Word. God's word spoken and written by the prophets was fulfilled by God's speech in Christ. The mysterious reality of speech revelation issuing out of God's very being is most profoundly expressed in the declaration that the Word of the creation became flesh and became also the source of the new redeemed community (Heb. 1:1-3; 11.3; John 1:1-14). Written or spoken, the breath of his mouth is life-creating and life-sustaining. The miracle of Pentecost and the Tongues is guarantee that the birth and power will be transmitted to the whole world.

This word is personal encounter, issuing out of the being of God, a laying hold by God of the one whom he addresses. With his word of power in grace, God's ends are achieved. God became the Immanent One who entered human life so that his creatures might enter his life. When that creature hid from God and formed an alliance with Satan, the estrangement was almost total; but in redemption, with infinite cost, God broke that alliance, reaffirmed the word that human beings bear God's image and are assigned to steward the earth, and established covenant with his people forever. The old revelation now radically enlarged and deepened continues as the first and major condition of restored religious covenant.

The second great condition of covenant relationship is human response to God's revelation. The counterpart of revelation is hearing and doing the word. In the Old Testament this is called the "fear of God" and in the New Testament, faith and obedience. That it must be a response not merely intellectual but in unique choice and in ultimate concern is indicated in what the Bible intends by "knowing" God. Such knowing is awareness of God and commitment to him at the depths of one's being; it is to choose him, to obey him, and to love him. As does God's self revelation, knowing in this Semitic sense entails intellectual dimensions, but is always more; it has to do with religious wholeness; it is a moral, emotional, spiritual, and action response as well as rational; and it issues from the center of a person's life.

Between revelation and knowing in this sense, there is a kind of "deep calling unto deep" (Psalm 42:7). It involves what Jewish theologian Martin Buber calls *I-Thou* encounter. Large parts of the Bible take on special religious significance when knowing is understood in that wholistic covenant sense. Thus God says: Let no one glory in anything except "that he understands and knows me" (Jer. 9:24). About judging for the poor and needy he asks, "Is not this to know me?" (Jer.22:15-16) He desires "the knowledge of God, rather than burnt offerings" (Hos. 6:6). "The fear of the Lord, that is wisdom; and to depart from evil is understanding" (Job 28:28). This knowing, the way from human beings to God, is in response to God's prior coming to us: "You only have I known of all the families of the earth" (Amos 3:2).

A closely related biblical meaning, that of the word "heart," reinforces the emphasis on the wholeness and the depth of covenant response. Scripture repeats many times that it is in the heart that one knows God; that out of the heart are the issues of life; that as one thinks in his heart so he is; that the heart rejoices in the Lord. The prophet says, "rend your hearts and not your garments," and in the Psalms the heart cries out for the living God. This emphasis on knowing God from the heart underlines the Bible's insistence that the objective scope of revelation needs, for religious closure, the corollary of subjective ultimate concern; human response must be a whole response to God's whole word of address in creation and redemption.

The requirement to know God in this moral and existential way emphasizes the important religious and educational reality that persons are free and responsible. The challenge of the probationary command in the garden as well as of Joshua was "Choose this day whom you will serve" (Josh. 24:15). At Sinai and in the prophets, the word is "obey the law." In the Sermon on the Mount, Jesus declares that he who hears and chooses to do his word builds on the rock (Matt. 7:24ff.). Human obedience is to be a living before the face of God. Rooted in the freedom of faith and love, religious responsibility becomes the freedom of significant moral choice.

Paul's writings emphasize such freedom in Christ and the Christian's responsibility to live up to this freedom. Justification by faith was for the sake of the consummation of religious relationship. Persons restored to God through faith in Christ must henceforth live as a new creation in a religious life related to the breadth of Christ's redemption. Paul related the obligation and possibility of covenant life to Christ's fulfilling the Old Testament—not the abandonment of the old but its consummation. The purpose of Christ's coming in the fullness of time was that he, having created all things, came to reclaim and restore all things (Col.1:15-20). It is the restoration of God's covenant with the man and the woman.

The crucial matter for both religion and education is this biblical view of calling in the world. Whether in Paul, in the prophets, in the Sinaitic law, or in the revelation at creation, human calling is the same: to respond to God and to all of reality religiously, at the depths of life and in all of life. Christ's work and our response to it do not destroy or annul history and the human and natural conditions of life, nor change our comprehensive calling within this world. Rather, his work fulfills and gives religious significance to "all things" with and through which we worship and work.

In addition to this biblical evidence on the scope of religion and its covenantal aspects, the religious question for education needs answers about biblical perspectives on the qualities and calling of human beings; on nature, culture, and stewardship; and on history and significant moral choice.

The Qualities and Calling of Persons

As has been noted earlier, human increased endowments and capacities made possible and required a special kind of response to God. Although part of nature and related to it, human beings, unlike birds and trees and stars, were also in God's image (Gen.1:27). Made of the dust of the ground, they were united with all that was physical. The command to be fruitful and to multiply united them with all living things whose existence would be extended through living seed. The breath of life in their nostrils united them with all that was animal. But human persons were also different. The mystery and challenge was that this difference would manifest itself within the bounds of relatedness to the earth and to all its creatures.

In the biblical record, human creation receives special attention. Of no other creature was the plan to create announced and the process described as in the human case. The difference is emphasized in the declaration, "In the image of God he created them," and in the giving of an assignment, "dress the garden, develop the earth, be in charge over all things." God created human persons to live in three relationships: they are part of the world of creatures; they are "in charge" of nature and its creatures; and they are tied to God in religious stewardship. The endowments given to humankind which make possible these relationships—physical-psychological, rational-moral-creative, and religious-spiritual endowments—are to function not as separate faculties, but interrelatedly and inseparably in life in the world under God. In such wholeness, human beings find their unique place between nature and God. To see the infinite difference between God as creator and nature as creation, yet not to deny either one nor to affirm either one alone, is the challenge and tension of human calling.

As has been developed previously, the Bible emphasizes calling primarily as a response in religious relationship. It is to be a whole response, not only with respect to the various areas of human life, but also with respect to the various functions of human nature. Within nature and in history, humankind's specific mandate was to dress the garden and have sovereignty.

What would life in response to such a calling be like? The mandate was all-encompassing: to establish family, society, government; to develop language, laws, and philosophy; to make dams and churches, poems and art, science and music, schools and bridges, ships and houses. All the fullness of earth was theirs, for appreciation and for work, to use their endowments as cultural beings. At the same time, it was first of all God's. Human sovereignty was both a derived and a responsive sovereignty; it was to be a stewardship under God, with religious accountability. This accountability meant not only that they might not exploit or ravage the earth; and not only that they be true to themselves as part of the earth, and to the world as their proper home. Stewardship under God meant that they were to be religious in work and governance and culture; that they offer work as a sacrifice of devotion to God. Significance and sanctity were not to be sought by making life a ladder or "means to" something above and beyond the world. The stewardship was one of religion in the world; they were to live in covenant with God in the midst of life and work and culture, and to hallow all of it. The Bible's emphasis on tithing, on first fruits, on the anointing of kings, on the religious aspects of diet, and similar associations of spiritual with physical are evidence of this biblical perspective.

The difference by which God set human beings off from the rest of creation, from trees and stars and animals, was that they were not only physical but were, above all, rational, moral, and creative in a spiritual wholeness. Being in the image of God determined that human beings could worship God and should do so. The capability to comprehend God's word and to respond to it made them able to change this "should" of obligation and this "could" of possibility into voluntary religious response in the covenant life with God.

The radical changes brought about by the fall and restoration neither abrogated God's covenant with the man and the woman nor changed their assignment to the earth. History is still God's history, from creation to the consummation, and humankind's place in that history is to live freely and responsibly within nature and within community. The assignment is now carried out under the burden of the sin-grace tensions, and the original covenant exists now under the signature of reconciliation through grace in Christ; but the religious duty in the midst of life, in nature and in history, is still the same appointment as in the beginning: to have charge of earth's fullness in the name of the Lord whose it is and to live in covenant relationship with him.

Biblical Perspectives on Nature

The Bible emphasizes throughout that the created reality of nature and the uncreated reality of God are infinitely and qualitatively distinct; yet it assigns great worth and significance to nature, to the physical conditions of life, and to the world which humankind was to make home. This biblical perspective disallows the error of making nature ultimate; it no less disallows the rejection of nature. God who alone is ultimate created nature and gave it great importance.

The Bible's view of the physical and natural is far from the dualistic notion that matter is evil and is therefore opposed to spiritual reality. God who is pure spirit takes delight in his physical creation; he said repeatedly that it was good (Gen. 1). God is concerned about sparrows and flowers, and he reveals his greatness in the universe. "All things" having been created by him, they are also redeemed by him (many Pss.; Isaiah 6:3; Col. 1:16-19). Jesus shows his respect and love for the natural not only in his familiarity with nature's ways and his constant use of nature parables, but also in his prodigal healing of sick and broken bodies, quite apart, in most cases, from any commitment of faith or obedience (Matt. 4:23; 8:16; 9:35; 14:36).

Another general pointer to the Bible's high view of the natural and physical is the frequent description of religious realities in terms of physical realities or metaphors. Human sin becomes real as a physical act; redemption is accomplished in a physical birth, death, and resurrection. Abraham is promised a land flowing with milk and honey, where his seed will be linked to the soil. The prophets extend this to a vision of God's people inheriting the whole earth. In the New Testament Jesus speaks of kingdom blessedness in the same terms, quoting the Old Testament. The language of the Revelation of St. John is overwhelming in its natural and physical allusions.

The Bible's emphasis on the physical world and on the natural conditions of life as God's creation and as God's concern is an emphasis on wholeness, one which gives the basis for keeping the physical and the spiritual in closest relation. This emphasis is of

51

great importance for Christian education, for a Christian view of culture, and for comprehensive religion. It forbids the disruptive dualisms between body and spirit, nature and grace, *this* world of experience and *that* world of revelation, which so persistently tempt or threaten Christians in their attitudes to the world. Rather, it means, as Martin Buber says, that a person chooses or rejects God "not in a relationship of faith empty of the content of this world, but in one which contains the full content of every day" (*Israel and the World*, p.17).

A model for the biblical view of physical and spiritual wholeness is suggested in the law-giving at Sinai. The provisions of these laws, temporary though many of them were, reflect important biblical principles for a covenant response of wholeness within both the spiritual and natural aspects of life. This wholeness is shown in that fact that in closest relation to the moral and ceremonial laws several other kinds of laws having to do with natural and civil matters are given. If the Ten Commandments were a call to religion in its ultimate form as fellowship with God, the ceremonial laws were reminders of the necessary temporal and spatial aspects of religion. And laws dealing with the social-economic spheres extend the covenantal duty to neighbor, society, and nature. This emphasis supports the general biblical view that religious response in the covenant was to be indivisible. We are to know God from the heart, in a subjective wholeness, but also in relation to comprehensive objective reality, in this case the vast natural-physical reality. In the practice of such wholeness we learn that we can possess our souls "spiritually" only by responding to God in the totality of life, in time and in the world. We are to learn, to quote Buber again, that the Bible is "serious about the appointment of man to earth" (*Israel and the World*, p. 16). What is found in the theocratic organization of Israel's national life reflects what God had instituted at creation, within human nature and in humanity's cultural and religious mandates.

Although there appear to be suggestions in the Bible that the physical in human beings is the seat of sin, this is in fact not a biblical teaching. Rather, it is the sinful spirit of humankind that controls the flesh. The sin of Eve was motivated predominantly by the unholy spiritual desire to be as God (Gen.3:5-6). The real meaning of Paul's "flesh" is not body but the carnal principle within the "old man," a principle of worldliness and of pride and power. Although gross physical sins appear to suggest moral bondage to the flesh, the Bible makes clear that it is the evil heart that corrupts the body. Thus the call to desist from sin without any corresponding call to deny the body and the promises of physical restoration in the Psalms and prophets suggest that escape not from the body or the world but from the *mind* of the flesh, from the evil spirit of human beings, was the way of salvation.

Salvation was to be in, under, and with the physical. Although a violated garden of Eden was closed to the man and the woman, its reopening was promised; although the flood brought destruction, the covenant of nature confirmed God's faithfulness; although child-bearing was in pain, children were a "heritage of the Lord;" and the earth would one day be restored in a new heaven and earth. According to the Bible, sin reaches deeply into nature and into man's physical life, but is not seated there. It is seated in the heart; out of the heart, Proverbs says, the issues of life come forth, including sin (Prov. 4:23).

The appearance of dualism between body and spirit, or later between nature and grace, falls away before these considerations. Both revelation and response deeply involve nature. Comprehensive religion results in part from the biblical celebration of the natural. Covenant blessings are often described in terms of inheriting the earth, receiving a land flowing with milk and honey, and of souls delighting themselves in physical abundance. The consummation described by John in the most lavish physical concreteness did not give offense to believers but was accepted as a symbol and guarantee of blessedness to come. The Song of Solomon is a celebration of life in its natural fullness; the splendor of the temple is a delight to the Lord; and costly perfume spilled in worship of Christ is not rebuked but accepted.

This is not to deny that Christians must transcend the physical and find their life with God at the depths of their hearts, in faith, and in the transcendent dimensions of hope and courage and inner peace. There are times when they are called to self-denial and even to world-renunciation. Christians are to be not possessors but stewards of the natural gifts of life. Even so, purpose and stewardship are in the midst of the historical, the natural, and the human conditions of life. Not a denial but an affirmation of the physical is the biblical way. Most of the time, for most people in the normal course of life, "There is nothing better than that he should make his soul enjoy good in his labor. This also I saw, that it was from the hand of God" (Eccl. 2:24).

The great significance and worth of the natural as the Bible sets it forth becomes comprehensible only in relation to the human person as a physical-spiritual unity, body and soul, whom God crowns with glory and honor and makes ruler over the works of his hands (Psalm 8:4-6). The God-given Sabbath also is for the benefit of both body and soul. A day for physical rest, it is also a day for religious delight and renewal, for the hallowing of human work and purpose and calling in the world. It is a symbol of both human union with nature and human transcendence of the physical.

The most significant biblical testimony to the importance of the natural and physical comes in the Bible's story of reconciliation. The *fact* of the incarnation, that is, the great mystery of Christ's assumption of physical, natural humanity, forever exalts the worth and significance of human nature. The *purpose* of redemption is to restore sinful persons but also "all things" which Christ had himself created, including all the physical, natural, and human orders and relationships of life. The *manner* of redemption was by Christ's identifying with nature itself, being born of a woman, uniting himself with human sin and guilt, and accomplishing reconciliation in his physical, natural death on the cross. The *completion* of the redemption comes in resurrection and ascension of Christ in his body and in his human nature, and through the resurrection of the bodies of believers. In all of these ways the Bible's high view of the natural dimensions of human existence is confirmed and enlarged.

Neither does the gospel mandate, which redemption initiates, repudiate nature or abrogate the cultural mandate. People are called to repent and to believe—and to return to their daily work in and through nature. For this they were given mind and hands and the creative will to culture. This is their religious calling, according to the Bible, and requires that nature be honored and cherished. That calling to cultural responsibility in nature needs special emphasis, particularly in relation to religion in education. For as in sin human beings often deny their stewardship under God by making nature or culture ultimate, so in grace they are tempted to deny this calling by being only "spiritual" and otherworldly, and by turning their backs upon nature and culture and history. Such a dualism or dichotomy the Bible does not permit. Covenant means to be religious within the totality of the natural and human conditions of life.

But then this too must be emphasized: according to that same covenant the world is to be transcended. The Bible shows that people are to find the meaning and purpose of life in God's purpose, in the "divine history." Their stewardship is placed in the service of the kingdom of God. In meeting the challenge to live as spiritual persons, as unique individuals, men and women reach their full humanness, related to both natural and spiritual reality, and in this way they become participators in God's history.

Biblical Perspectives on History

In the biblical perspective human beings in history are persons responsible in freedom, under the sovereignty of God. God's sovereignty in nature and in grace directs human history to the coming of Christ's kingdom, and people have the dual obligation (a) to acknowledge this sovereignty and (b) at the same time to grow as unique individuals through significant moral choices. Order and freedom so related are the ultimate religious conditions of human historical life. Faith in Jesus Christ and covenant obedience to God involve not escape from but rather acceptance of the complexities, ambiguities, and moral tensions of historical life, and religious response to them in personal freedom and choice.

The Bible presents history as God's history but also humanity's. God's law and purpose confront persons, and they respond in reverence and obedience. God controls all things, yet human actions are new, unique, and decisive. Within the mystery of these two realities, each individual as doer and agent in history is free and responsible. His calling requires that he be loyal and self-giving in nature and society but also that he transcend nature and society when this is required by God's history. Persons must live deeply, responsibly, creatively within the structures and establishments of society without letting them be ultimate. Religious stewardship in the case of history requires commitment to what in the Bible is gradually revealed as the universal redemptive community of the kingdom of God.

In facing the claims of this community over against the rival claims of secular or idolatrous substitutes for it, as well as the rival claims of temporary and proximate manifestations of it, religious persons are called to be free individuals before God. Abraham and Saul of Tarsus gave up their societies for God's history not because they understood God's plan but because they heard his command. Theirs is the company of those who never give ultimate allegiance to passing institutions, whether religious or secular, but remain open to God's will and purpose. Such persons discover that the essence of life in the covenant, life between law and freedom, is being called upon to choose God again and again, and in such choice growing as religious persons. It is *growth* because such choices between God and god are made within the concreteness of the natural and historical conditions of life and, in that flow, are unrepeatable.

In the biblical view, then, moral tensions and crises are normal to the people of God. Human failure to choose, the proneness to prefer the security of status and position to the risks of moral commitment, as well as demonic choices against God, constitute sin. It is the choice of Satan's history instead of God's history. The conflict, the antithesis, if you will, between these two histories is announced in Genesis after the fall, and is the theme of the Bible from Paradise lost to the consummation. It is because human beings are capable of real choice that they are able to resist God's plan for history. A prominent biblical example is the irreligious traditionalism against which both the prophets and Jesus directed their strongest opposition—as a result of which the prophets were stoned and Jesus was crucified. Foreign alliances, golden calves, reducing religion from existential covenant-keeping to cult and ceremony, failure to accept God's movement to "the uttermost parts of the earth"—against all such deviations and sinful conformities, God calls the covenant people to their true destiny: to be to God a kingdom of priests and a holy nation, and so to build the kingdom of God.

Thus all of history in the biblical perspective is covenantal history, based on God's action and revelation according to his plan and on human response in moral choice to that action and revelation. Although the revelation is never total and human understanding is only partial and is marred by sin, men and women are nevertheless real participants in a real covenantal history, existing in a religious relationship with God. The biblical view of God in control of history, unlike non-biblical views, is not primarily that he represents a principle of meaning or rational structure of order, but rather that he is the holy and eternal One who is in relationship with men and women and with his creation. God's transcendent self-existence, power, and majesty are a covenant sovereignty, a sovereignty which imposes a special obligation to respond not only to power and majesty but to love, love in the original act of God in creation, with all of its gifts, but above all love in the redeeming act of God by which persons are saved from sin.

In the covenant God imposes restraints upon his own freedom with acts and promises and conditions in history; by drawing men and women into covenant he restricts their freedom by those same acts and promises. This restraint, however, frees them from license and autonomy and from the demonic results of sin. It is freedom to know the truth and to do it, to know God and to love him, to be bound to God and to choose him. These choices as cause and result help shape human history; by means of them persons grow as free individuals, and the kingdom of God comes into being each time anew, cumulatively and as community in human history.

Because God initiates history and directs it; because his law, his design, his sovereignty place him above any need or contingency (Deut. 32:39; Acts17:24-25); and because in nature and in grace, God is Lord over all, it would seem that man is neither free nor responsible. In the biblical view, however, before God he is both. Thus the fall of Adam and Eve, the call of Abraham, the exodus from Egypt, the organization of the theocracy, the great exiles, the crucifixion of Christ, the spread of the young church, and personal choice of Christ are all mighty acts of God; but in each case they either confront persons with genuine choices or are themselves the results of such choices. God employs human acts, individual and communal, to bring about his purposes. When, as in biblical history, these goals, by God's revelation and by human quest, become also a community goal, then individuals and community become genuine partners with God in history. God says to Israel: "If you will obey my voice and keep my covenant . . . you shall be to me a kingdom of priests and a holy nation" (Exod.19:5-6; 1 Peter 2:9; Rev. 21:3). Directed alike to Israel, to the New Testament church, and to the inhabitants of Paradise restored in the consummation, this word was first spoken to the man and the woman in the creation covenant.

This mystery of divine-human relationship is confirmed throughout the Bible in the significance assigned to human choices and in the responsibility assigned to people for them: in the original choice in the fall; in the choice persons are commanded to make concerning Christ; and in all the subordinate and related choices to which the long biblical record witnesses. The word in Joshua's farewell address declares it unambiguously; in the context of a dramatic recital of God's sovereign acts on their behalf, he challenges Israel to "choose this day whom you will serve" (Josh. 24:15). God's control of history does not lift men and women out of history or leave them puppets in time; it thrusts them into life as participants in the lived dialogue. The "solution" of the mystery of human freedom before God's sovereignty lies in accepting covenantal existence in history and never denying either of the opposed terms.

Such covenantal living becomes possible through the revelation of God's united law and love. Law and love in conjunction create and compel an obedience which, though it begins in constraint, issues in covenant. Law and love call his people to know God in a comprehensive life orientation and in ultimate concern. They both guarantee and challenge human freedom.

In the historical tensions between God's order and human freedom, sin and grace find their central place in the covenant. Sin is a denial of human responsibility before God's law and his love, and grace results in a re-acceptance of that responsibility, a restoration to the privileges and obligations of covenant. Grace emphasizes that law and responsibility are the basis of true religion and real history. Only if this is understood can the biblical emphasis on love and obedience, whether at Sinai, in the prophets, in the Gospels, or in the Epistles, be understood. Grace, according to the Bible, is for those who choose God in response to his choice of them. Such mutual choosing guarantees that persons will choose God's goals for history, goals having to do with one's relation to his neighbor and one's relation to the kingdom of God. Making this choice, one is not to be diverted by the claims of society, of existing establishments (secular or religious), or of the familiar and comfortable structures of life. Rather, personal love to one's neighbor and personal loyalty to the kingdom of God are precisely that which the movement of history and individual fulfillment as human beings require.

According to the Bible, humankind's ultimate religious concern is to see neighbor and society, community and history, in their inter-relationships and wholeness, and to respond to them as part of a covenantal relationship to God. That response begins with repentance and faith and God's forgiveness, but it goes on for each person in his life with his neighbor and in daily work in society and culture. Christian schools can be the community's expression of such ultimate religious concern; as such, they will be the embodiments and agents of comprehensive religion.

Note: In the original, this material is followed by the educational applications now in Chapter Ten.

CHAPTER FIVE

Unpacking Covenant
for Our Day

All of reality—everything that is created,
God himself, and all of history—
gives us the conditions of religious response.

As long as there have been Christian schools in the Reformed community, here and in The Netherlands, we have spoken of them as covenantal schools; yet this language has remained a verbalism as far as educational theory and practice go. I believe that a clarification of the notion of covenant will take educators and parents, both in and outside the Reformed tradition, beyond slogans and abstractions with respect to both religion and education. I will argue that the profoundly relevant biblical metaphor of covenant is able to do three things for us: place Christian schools squarely in the main stream of contemporary concern for whole religion and whole religious involvement; drive Christian communities back to a biblical and Protestant theology of relationship between God and humankind; and re-establish the idea of world view rooted in the depth dimension of faith and ultimate commitment.

The covenant metaphor for religious relationship seems particularly suited to the kind of religious language and religious concern that have become current in contemporary theology and culture (as suggested in Chapter Four). Insights into biblical theology by outstanding thinkers of our day in the Christian and in the Jewish traditions make it possible to employ both the idea and the word covenant in remarkably relevant ways. In both its biblical sense and in contemporary religious "existential" applications, the idea of covenant supports a comprehensive life-orientation, involving the question of this-worldliness in relation to other-worldliness. Thus it will directly bear on education to the extent that the educational question is seen to be first of all a religious question.

In contemporary concern for whole religion and for human vocation to and within the secular world, the idea of covenant is prominent. This emphasis can bring a new awareness of the utility of the covenant metaphor for expressing the biblical framework of world-and-life view on the one hand, and personal response in passion and commitment on the other. And through this awareness the educational corollaries of *teaching* and *learning* may also be better understood and begin to get better content and statement.

Tracing in the Bible a pattern of covenant development (as in Chapter Four) gives an entrance into Old Testament history and into the early chapters of Genesis—without which the Old Testament remains not much more than a series of revolving doors to those who read it. In this development there is a kind of chart, or at least a compass fix, for travel through the Old Testament and on into the fulfillment in New Testament times and writings. There is also a chart of sorts for a Christian view of history and cultural involvement in the New Testament age—until the Lord returns.

We should further note that the biblical idea of covenant distinguishes biblical religion from all other religions—from those religions whose God is far off, impersonally remote from the world and its people, and from those religions whose God is impersonally identified with the world and its people. The Christian biblical religion is not deist according to which a remote watchmaker God starts things and lets them run out. Nor is it pantheist, according to which all is God and God is all, an impersonal energy holding people and the cosmos together. In biblical religion, God is Creator and Sovereign over all, but his is a father's relational sovereignty; and he is Redeemer who in his Pentecostal coming and in the Holy Sacrament has pledged to live among and in his people forever.

The idea of covenant has sometimes been considered a private and somewhat shop-worn and disreputable hold-over from immigrant parents. Many who think of covenant only in the old words of the baptism vows, the parents' promise to instruct their children or "cause them to be instructed" in the faith, wonder what that awesome obligation has to do with schooling.

The answer depends almost entirely on how "big" we judge the Christian religion to be. At this point the grand Reformed slogans still work. The Christian religion, we say, entails a world-and-life view. Covenant means living always "before the face of God;" it entails kingdom obedience as both private morality and public word and action. Such living means not only being judgmental of all the sin and darkness in the world but also religiously celebrating all God's gifts in his creation and in human civilization through the ages.

Covenant Means Communion

If we read the Bible in a Reformed way, we will go beyond citing proof texts to use the methods of biblical theology. This means letting one part of the Bible clarify another part; it means seeing the historical progress of revelation and especially the core idea. That core is covenant from beginning to end. Not covenant in the usual limited meanings—baptism vows, comfort when a child dies, or admonition to behave "like covenant children"—but the I-Thou relationship, which is the golden thread through the whole Bible.

Covenant is the profound mystery of God in all his majesty and awesomeness coming into relation with people in all their fallenness. God the high and holy One in heaven, infinite in his perfections, announced in the thunder and lightning of Sinai—he is the One who stoops down into relationship with his image-bearers. He is the One who walked with Enoch, was the friend of Abraham, the husband of Israel, the shepherd of his people, the father of his children. Covenant is the mystery that climaxes in the coming of Jesus, Immanuel, God with us, in a stable, with angels singing *Gloria in excelsis*. Biblical religion is covenantal religion.

Covenant as I am speaking of it here is broader than the Redemptive Covenant, or Covenant of Grace. It includes the whole of God's condescending intercourse with human beings. It began when God created the man and the woman, with their first contemplation of God's works, all about them and within them, by which they knew directly God's everlasting power and divinity. There ensued, inevitably, communion between the God who created and the creature capable of response. After the fall God reached down in his sovereign grace to reclaim an alienated humanity. The Covenant of Grace, while new and different, is a reinstatement of the former one. To be sure, true knowledge is now generated by a special redemptive revelation of word and act; true righteousness is now wholly by grace and not by obedience; true holiness is now conceived and born of the Spirit, altogether supernaturally. But behind and over it all is this: that God reunites regenerate persons to himself in fellowship, in communion, in life. Paradise is restored. In the economy of redemption we have not a new, unrelated, closed finale to human history and destiny. We find rather that it is a restorative, redemptive episode. Redemption means the reinstatement, the re-establishment of the creation covenant.

This covenant means a mutuality between two parties, or better, two moral beings. The communion, the mutual giving of self, takes place between God and persons. In the Scripture we read of it: "I will be a God to you, and you shall be my people." Although the initiative is wholly with God, and although God assigns the covenant and its conditions unilaterally, it nevertheless means genuine communion between two moral natures, the divine uncreated and the human created. It was loving and condescending on God's part, religious on humanity's part. This the Reformed creeds express when they speak of "knowing God and enjoying Him."

To speak of such communion is at once to speak of its basis, of that which makes communion possible: the Image of God in his creature. The pre-redemptive communion between God and persons was a corollary of their creation by God as rational-moral beings, after his own likeness. It is this which constitutes the human as more than animal. Human beings are rational, and moral, and free, and immortal, and responsible. The creature, as created, possessed true knowledge, righteousness, and holiness. There was and is a reflection of God himself in man and woman. The Image of God makes communion possible, but also inevitable—from God's side by free intention, from humanity's side by increated destiny.

Having thus in the beginning made the man and the woman as his supreme creatures for a life of communion with him, God provided for it in two ways: he showed himself to them, spoke to them, communicated with them; and he created them in such a way that they could receive, understand, be affected by, and respond to his Word. God's self-giving in the creation covenant required each person's response and commitment in all of life, all the time. God's covenantal commands were three: to love God above all in true worship; to love each other in true community; and, under the controls of those loves, to do the world's work.

This creation covenant is also the line which the redemptive covenant, after the fall, does not break or change but restores and guaranties. Old Testament religious encounter and response, under grace, illustrate this and are needed to give shape and force to New Testament religion. Covenant represents the whole circle of life within which the cross is central. That is, the circle is the main thing, a circle of life in which the cosmic Christ and his redemption radiates out to the periphery at a hundred points, each radius marking off human domains in which Christ declares, It is mine!

Because covenant relationship in the Bible is such a relationship of giving and receiving at the depths of life, it is a relationship also that develops and unfolds, that *grows*. It grows by facing outward—toward the range and variety and complexity of human life in the world, the world of neighborliness and community, and the world of work and culture. It grows by obeying the cultural mandate. Covenant means that such facing outward is not separate from, next to, or lower than relationship to God; covenant means that such facing outward is all bound up with the true worship of God. The man and the woman could perceive and respond to God's word in the whole creation, in all that he had made—in all the arrangements, order, laws, and mysteries of what we today call the sciences, both human and natural sciences. Because of their marvelous endowments as image-bearers they were able to respond to God's encountering them in all these ways. Through such extensive relationships the intensive relationship of covenant grows and matures into the life with God, which is the essence of covenant religion.

Covenant, Kingdom and Education

In talk about covenant and about Christian schooling the words kingdom of God are often heard. Covenant life with God may be spoken of as life in the kingdom; some vocations are called "kingdom work;" and Christian schools are pledged to advance that kingdom. It is important therefore to explore its meaning.

That kingdom, through Christ and the Holy Spirit, is a gift and not an achievement. Yet in the mystery of grace-and-obedience, its members are bidden by Jesus to work for what they ask for when they pray "Your kingdom come on earth." That kingdom is not only future, as some fundamentalists say, but also a present reality. It is present not only in people's hearts but also publicly. It is public not only in individuals but also communally in God's people united. It is communal not only in the church but also in Christians living in ordinary society as Christ's disciples.

And so for Christians the kingdom comes in business, in the arts, in hospitals, in science, in politics, in day labor—and in schools. It comes in all these areas because "our world belongs to God." It belongs to him twice over, through creation and through redemption. Over this world Jesus now reigns because it was by him that all things were created (John 1), through him all things are redeemed (Col. 1), and to him all authority in heaven and on earth has been given (Matt. 28).

In their daily living Christ's men and women acknowledge Christ's authority in two ways: in celebrating life in God's world, physical and cultural, and in transforming all that sin has made ugly and evil. Because such two-fold discipleship is complex, young persons need a certain kind of Christian education that will help them in their present day-by-day living and prepare them for adult life.

When parents seek "kingdom education" for their children, they are seeking education for that intensive and extensive covenant obedience. Such education is rooted in creation, not in redemption. The church and Christianity are concerned with it because redemption *restores* creation institutions (like family, society, and government). As a creation institution, education is religiously occupied with the cultural mandate: with man in society, in history, and with all things natural and human. This is not merely an addendum to the great commission of Matthew 26, and therefore of secondary urgency, but is the inescapable corollary of covenantal religious concern. For these reasons, Christian schools should aim to be *schools* in the best tradition of schools—based upon and giving expression to covenantal religion in the best tradition of the Bible.

In the beginning, when God created the man and the woman, he created also education. Their work of making culture out of nature involved education. As his image-bearers, they were structured, fortified, and endowed, unlike the trees and stars and animals, with gifts for understanding and choosing to obey his directions. Schooling for themselves and for their children was not an add on—it was in the nature of things. In the creation covenant restored by Christ we have the *why* of Christian schools: the cultural mandate to do the world's work; we have the *what:* all that God has revealed in nature, history, society, self, and the Bible; and we have the *how*: the capacities, the mind, will, and imagination, of God's image bearers.

I think it follows then that in order for regenerate humankind to attain progressively the true holiness, or communion of life, which the Covenant still intends for us and our children today, we shall in our education have to reckon diligently with all of general revelation, always under the light and discipline of special revelation, and we must underline for children their duty to and capacity for the endless adventure of more knowledge of God and more willing commitment to him. Learning increasingly to know God from his works in history, in nature, and in human personality, and increasingly choosing for that God in every situation of thought and conduct—these are the covenantal requirements upon us all. These constitute the core need of the personalities in our classrooms.

For this reason I plead on covenantal grounds for education of the whole child, the child possessed of the Image of God, the child in process of both restoration and maturation. Through education in theology, in the humanities, and in science, the child will come to know God, to know himself or herself, to know his neighbor, and to know the world about her. These studies will mature the child as human, religiously human. Such education will fulfill the purpose of covenant: the perfection of the creature and the glory of the Creator, perpetuated in an everlasting communion between them.

CHAPTER SIX

The Perennial Problem

To be Reformed is to be affirmational:
the earth is the Lord's;
every bush is on fire.

What does the Christian have to do with "the world"? What is our place, our role, our calling in the work and progress of civilization? What do we believe about Christ and culture?

Liberal theologies of culture have answers that lack the depth dimension of experiential religion; fundamentalist theologies of conversion lack a comprehensive engagement with human culture. I believe we must find the answer to this "enduring problem" (as H. R. Niebuhr called it) in a large and vital Calvinism that combines the private religious rootage of a creed such as the Heidelberg Catechism with the involvement of our world-and-life view. I believe that Christians must articulate the biblical answer in a way that acknowledges worldly obedience as religious obligation until the Lord returns. That articulation is required in our discussion of economics, of the arts, of social problems, and, most dramatically, in our discussions about educating young Christians. The idea of Christian education is rooted in such a biblical answer.

I take it that Protestant and Catholic Christians in education can support each other reciprocally and productively in a common and enriching perception of the sort of wholeness Christian education ought above all to be concerned about. That wholeness goes beyond just general nurture and piety, and entails a comprehensive life orientation. We must face the ancient question of Tertullian: What has Jerusalem to do with Athens? and answer it, not in his way, rejecting culture. Nor must it be in the facile way of Tertullian's contemporary Cyprian—the way of accommodation to Athens, of blurring the momentous differences between degenerate and regenerate persons.

Rather, we must answer in our own twentieth century way. It must be the way of a Christian, biblical perspective on life and the world. It is the way of believing, affirming, and making educationally relevant a common Christian answer to the "Christ and culture" question. This question asks not *whether* Christ and culture are intimately related—whether faith and history are related, whether Sunday and Wednesday are related, whether science and exegesis are related, whether the child's physical and spiritual worlds are related. The answer to Tertullian's question is not *whether* they are related but *how*, accepting their inseparableness, we must articulate that relatedness and embody it in educational decisions.

The Biblical Basis

Previous chapters have indicated the biblical support for such an affirmational approach to Christianity and culture; it is found in the witness of the whole Bible to what humankind's relationship to God ought to be like. The Bible's word about religion is preeminently about redemption, but about redemption rooted in creation; it is about the gospel age, but about the gospel interlaced through history; it is about the Matthew mandate to preach repentance and reconciliation, but about repentance and reconciliation of prodigals who may not hide away as hired servants downstairs. Restoration of his sons and daughters into the Father's house means they must again accept the Genesis mandate to affirm the world and do the Lord's work. Covenant fidelity to the Lord over all requires that.

Although often ignored nowadays in discussions of Christian philosophy of education, the so-called cultural mandate of Genesis should be the control belief behind theorizing about Christian schooling.

It is possible that Adam asked, when he looked about him, "Lord, why? Why am I here?" What words were given then—words so momentous that they needed to be preserved, passed on during the years and generations, and one day—those words of the many spoken as the man and the woman walked with God in the Garden—written down in a book? Whether in answer to a specific question or not, they were words of reply, of clarification, of charge: What I want of you, Adam, is that you become a worker in the world for the enlargement of our life together and for the fulfillment of your life as human. You and the woman shall have children to fill the earth one day. Why are you, your children and their children here? The reason is: to do the world's work, to be cultural beings.

Those words in Genesis sum it up—for them and for us: This is your mandate: Dress the garden, cultivate the earth, have sovereignty over all things. The mandate was to make culture within nature; it was to grow in humanness by serving God in the fullness of daily life.

The world was humankind's to revel in and to steward. Trees upon the earth and the treasure within it; fish in the seas and cattle on a thousand hills; beasts of the forest and flowers in the fields. Over all of it they were to rejoice and for it to praise God. Beyond that, they were to work. They were to apply mind and imagination, heart and hand, to the data and givens of nature, unfolding and developing them for the enrichment and advancement of their human existence. They were to establish family and society and government; to develop language, laws, philosophy; as workers and creators they were to make dams and poems, science and music, art and bridges, ships and houses and factories. Though they were part of nature through body and breath and fertility, they were also image of God. They were to use their endowments as cultural persons.

This biblical calling to cultural work and responsibility extends our religious involvement to a range and complexity that are almost overwhelming. Constantly we are tempted to back off, to retreat to the simpler life. If the domain of business and economics is not really neutral or secular but bursting with religious ultimate concern, how do we find our way? If the arts are really not indifferent religiously except for questions of overt morality, how do we go about a Christian aesthetics, not only for critique, but also for the production of art? And what of human sexuality, human rights, environmental protection, economic and political justice, prison reform? In all these domains, we are called to engagement.

Objectors to the Genesis Mandate

Many evangelicals and many ecologists have in common these days that they don't go much for talk about the Genesis cultural mandate, though their reservations are of different magnitudes and have little in common. They are *other-worldly* evangelicals and *sub-worldly* ecologists—by worldly here I mean living up to the hilt in the midst of the natural-human-cultural-religious conditions of the Christian's earthly pilgrimage. When our Lord said, You are in the world but not of the world, he was also implying, as does biblical theology generally, that the only way and the only place we have of being not of the world, is *in the midst of the world*. Like it or not, we are worldly Christians; like it or not, we are called to a worldly holiness. So, too, like it or not, this reality of our existence is not a concession, given grudgingly by God or acquiesced in grudgingly by homesick saints. The reality and, yes, the dissonance, of our "worldliness" is that it is to be exalted in, to be celebrated, exercised, and proclaimed. This biblical answer, in the creation-redemption perspective, is inhospitable to all forms of liberal culture-religion on the one hand and to fundamentalist dualisms on the other.

Evangelical perspectives

Whether through benign neglect, hostile assertion, or arrested theology, many evangelicals (including many in Reformed churches) are "Christ against culture" Christians. It is not only that they are suspicious of secular culture and any sort of concourse or cooperation with unbelievers. They also easily move to a denial of the religious significance of the natural, cultural, and historical conditions of human existence. Daily work, symphony orchestras, poverty programs, Shakespearean scholarship, political participation, possessions, sex, food, mathematics—in their view, all are secular, secondary, inferior. They are in the domain of nature. As such, they are judged to be either ethically antithetical to things of the spirit (the nature-grace dualism), or metaphysically of a different order of reality than soul-spirit realities (the body-soul dualism). Though such evangelicals enter into activities within all these domains, they regard them at best as way-stations on their way out of this world.

Contrariwise, being mainly New Testament Christians, what they affirm is that the gospel mandate of Matthew is their ultimate concern, their real mandate. The other sorts of things may be permitted with care and caution, but are not required. What is required are the things relating directly to the gospel mandate: repentance, conversion, witnessing, Christian mercy, full-time kingdom work. Confronted with talk about the cultural mandate of Genesis, they are not only unmoved; they find in such talk a threat—perhaps a personal threat to their theological maturity but more often than not a threat to Christian orthodoxy itself. And then dialogue becomes difficult.

But if such evangelicals will listen, what does the other kind of Christian, the kind who wants to take creation and humankind's place and work in the world seriously, say to them about the significance of history, about Christian discipleship, and about a whole Bible's message? Because what I am writing about is the keystone in Christian education, let me put it this way: What do I say in a Philosophy of Education course?

This Christian brother or sister has a profound point when he or she says there is a lot of phony talk about Christians and culture. Christians compromising their faith in the name of cultural acquiescence and cooperation is one of the oldest offenses against the gospel—and against the doctrine of the cultural mandate. Casual Christians have all too readily, in the name of this doctrine, ignored the antithesis between truth and falsehood, light and darkness, the new man and the old man, God's work in the world and Satan's sabotage of that work.

This accommodation happens in local politics, in academic and professional societies, in the arts and sciences, in labor unions, and among rebellious young people. For perspective, admit that the accommodation goes on no less among respectable employers, medical associations, suburban housewives, scholars of economics or evolution, and in a cavalier identification by many evangelicals of Christianity with "the American way." The problem of accommodation and of seeing the antithesis between God's way and Satan's way is a difficult one.

Probably the most difficult objection when one speaks of cultural mandate is this one: Does not teaching the Genesis mandate of cultural obedience and dominion take too little account of man's fall—and of the critical need for preaching the gospel? Does the gospel mandate not replace, or at the very least take precedence over, the pre-fall cultural mandate? And, considering our focus on the education of the young, add this concern: Because of the fall and sin and the good news of salvation, should not the gospel mandate and not the other be written large above the doors to every Christian school?

The biblical answer, I believe, is that the gospel mandate of Matthew does not rescind the cultural mandate of Genesis nor does it become merely another mandate next to the old one, leaving it to Christians to choose between "spiritual" and "secular" work—shall they become pastors, missionaries, Christian school teachers, lay witnesses, or whatever else is implied by the expression "full time kingdom work," or choose to be doctors, plumbers, scholars, car-salesmen, or whatever else might be considered legitimate "secular" vocations? The biblical answer is that the Matthew mandate is *in order to* fulfill the other mandate: the Genesis mandate is part of the whole biblical story. Gospel is restoration to creation covenant. Every vocation is in service to God.

The answer to other-worldly evangelicals must be that the Christian life is to be lived neither in fearful withdrawal from society's ordinary life nor in uncritical accommodation to that life. It is to be a life of Christian discipleship in which both work and worship become a celebration of the reality that through creation and redemption the earth and its fullness as well as human life and its fullness are the Lord's. Though in the fall covenant was broken, though in sin human beings are alienated from God, from their fellow human beings, and from their world, Christ restored "all things." He restores covenant, which can today be a viable frame of reference for the question about Christ and culture; he restores image of God, the endowments for relationship to God; and he restores human calling in this world.

In this view of things, we accept each new day as a gift for doing the world's work. We accept life's common problems and challenges as part of our being religiously called in and to the world. Moreover, we accept this challenge along with non-Christians as our common work in the world. Sometimes together, sometimes alone, we do the work of the human community, open to all persons as fellow creatures of God, living together in nature and in history. Not withdrawal from humankind but openness, concern, involvement is the biblical way.

Of course, this view of life presents threats and risks. The antithesis between God's cause and Satan's cause pulls us now this way, now that way. The answer must be not that we bury our talents but that we live by faith and obedience. It means never forgetting that even the saint can fall away, but that we must nevertheless plant our trees and light our candles. It means that although we are pilgrims, seeking the eternal city, we must as God's men and women be his representatives and do his work in humankind's common society and common history.

If we ever needed Christian schools, we need them today. We need them for promoting a clear and steady religious outlook, a public Christianity—for our own young Christians, for the Christian community, and for the nation at large. Such a religious vision will expose what Bonhoeffer called "cheap grace," the easy discipleship, the sentimental verbal witnessing to having Jesus as our buddy. It will help nurture mature young Christians who don't have all the answers but are learning what the questions are, learning that the questions are more complex than many will admit, and learning where to search for answers.

Ecological perspectives

What about the objections of ecologists to talk of a mandate for human sovereignty? What about the ill effects they cite?

Such abuse would seem to be prohibited by a "whole Bible" perspective which shows the cultural mandate rooted in and defined by covenant faithfulness—faithfulness to neighbor and to God—and thus to culture itself. The earth was first of all the Lord's. Human sovereignty was to be a derived and responsible sovereignty; the man and the woman were stewards under God. This cultural stewardship was part of their religious obligation. The probationary command and the two trees in the center of the garden became the immediate reminders of a transcendent order beyond themselves and the world, became memorials of their covenant with God and their religious accountability.

Accountability is important. It not only forbids exploitation, ravaging, or desecrating the earth. It asks that man and woman honor the earth as their proper home. Accountability meant they were to be religious in work and governance and culture; they were to offer these as a sacrifice of devotion to God; they were to begin and end each day in the consciousness that each day was the Lord's day.

Accountability also meant that stewardship in the natural and the hallowing of the natural were to be expressed not by lifting this life out of the world, by "spiritualizing" it, or by making it a means to some spiritual exercise. The stewardship was one of religion in the world; of finding God, who is transcendent and holy, in his creation; of living in covenant with God in the midst of life and work and culture; and of hallowing it all as religious obedience.

Christian education is very much about stewardship, understood in its biblical sense of religious accountability, allegiance, obedience. Christian education is about how the sense and consciousness of such stewardship is to be promoted in young persons in the schools. Such education has to do, as Joshua said, with choosing "this day whom you will serve" and impressing this requirement upon young persons, constraining them to choose at all the crossroads that a good curriculum presents to them.

Without such accountability to God, a catastrophe far more demonic than even ecologists can imagine despoils human life and world. That catastrophe reaches into our art, our politics, our families, our business, our church, our school—into every domain of our world. It is the catastrophe of sin, of rebellion, of fallenness. It is the catastrophe of our disoriented minds, of our disintegrated morality, of our miscreative self-expression. It is the catastrophe of our world and our endowments despoiled through serving not the living God but the idols of power, of pride, of pleasure, of possessions.

Christians need a renewed religious vision of worldly living, of worldly holiness in that life. Christian schooling, rooted in the biblical view of personhood and of human calling, must foster that vision, refocused for the learner in and through Jesus Christ by whom came and comes the restoration of all things. That vision must restore the religious meaning of stewardship—in ecology, to be sure, but also in the range and complexity of our whole life in the world. It must be a stewardship of rejoicing and celebration—and of willing accountability. Toward such religious stewardship a Christian school's curriculum and its learning goals must be directed.

The Way of Affirmation

In respect to Christian life in the world, the notion of "permission" is a wrong notion, and is not the first question to be asked. Whether to participate in film arts and scientific inquiry, in alleviating poverty or racism are questions not of permissibility but of obligation. A basic premise of Christian living is that we ask not what may we do, how close to the world may we go, but rather, what *ought* we to be doing. The question is: how do we as Christians live obediently within the whole complex of our natural, social, historical, cultural existence?

We should, then, first of all affirm culture, that is, affirm physical nature and human society, cultural stewardship and historical choices—as our proper and normal and expected stance in the world until the Lord returns. Because of pervasive evil and sin, we will at times resist the culture, sometimes cooperating with non-Christians, and much of the time working to transform things on every hand. But it will be in the mood of, in the signature of, first of all, affirming the original mandate. Going beyond the mind of fear and withdrawal, beyond also the mind of crisis, or that of personal morality and simple faith, and also beyond the notion of transformation, the positive mind is locked into culture and committed to it. Or let us say it is not so much a going *beyond* as a going *before*. The affirming mind is a stance that precedes and becomes the basis for transformation, for crisis action, and even, at times, for total separation.

Thus, our answer to "what does the Christian have to do with the world, with civilization, and with history?"—"what does Jerusalem have to do with Athens?"—should be not merely in the language of transformation, not merely in the language of engagement and debate and world improvement. Although this emphasis is of fundamental and continuing importance, what needs to be emphasized first is the Christian's rightful place in the world, the Christian's indefeasible citizenship in the world. We need to emphasize that we have not only the right to live here as our home, but the duty to live here; not only the duty but the privilege; not only the privilege to live here but the vocation to celebrate it, to praise and glorify God, to affirm the creation. It is our privilege and vocation to affirm not only the creation as the physical world of things and of plants and of people, but also creation as civilization itself, the domain of culture, whose great riches we inherit.

In Christian schools and communities we should, I suggest, speak not first of all of the transformation but rather of the affirmation of culture. The Lord's earth and its fullness are created and redeemed through Jesus Christ and, in stewardship authorized by God, they are now also yours and mine and our children's. Affirming the world, that's the biblical vision—not building ladders out of it. The Dutch writer A. Van Ruler says that unless we share God's joy in his world "we are not yet wholly the children of God." That is the tradition in which we call for Christian schooling.

Christ, Culture, and Education

Our slogans—world-and-life view, the glory of God, covenant, Christ is king over all—have served us well in some aspects of Christian schooling. But because we have taken these as a *last* word, we often failed to draw out the educational implications in the hard language of aims and method. Rather, these slogans must be the *beginning* of educational philosophy. Unless we re-interpret our slogans and get caught up with them as a theology of culture, the slogans will not really live and the educational applications will not seem terribly important.

The unique task of the school has everything to do with the cultural mandate. Without that emphasis you stop having a *school*. In a religious community's division of responsibilities, the school is a special case of formal teaching and learning. It uses a special kind of subject matter and methodology—such as are appropriate to the great blocks of time at its disposal, appropriate to the training and competency of teachers, and appropriate to the vast obligation placed upon it by the Christian community. The school is charged mainly with teaching the young the meaning of and obedience to the third great command: to do the work of the world.

Such a school is a good school when it transmits the Bible's religious vision and calling not apart from, or next to, but by means of its major aims and priority subject matter. It is a good school when with pedagogical concern and expertise it teaches young persons that Christian truth is not simple but complex; that Christian living is not easy but difficult; that believing in Jesus Christ is not a last word, but a first word. It is a good school when it teaches its students that the Christian life in God's world is a journey in the understanding, the choosing, and the actions of living in covenant with God; and when in all these ways it gives young persons "more to be Christian with." Especially in the school young persons learn that their life in the Spirit cannot be above or in any way apart from daily experience in the world. Rather, such a life must be incarnate within the natural, historical, and cultural conditions of their human existence.

At the same time, students must learn the Christian view of the second great commandment, finding and loving our neighbor in our common world. Of course, the great dividing exists: between faith and unbelief; between obedient stewardship and vain autonomy. That all-pervasive antithesis requires that Christians search out and expose the spiritual warfare within themselves and all around them, and that we proclaim the gospel in terms of that antithesis. But finding and loving the neighbor is predicated on mankind's human and historical solidarity. As long as time lasts, universal human community endures—remaining open to God's special grace through the mission of the church. Necessary for this is the Christian's openness to all persons, as fellow creatures of God but also as fellow aliens within fallen humankind who live together in nature and in history.

All of this the Christian school must teach. Rejecting on the one hand ascetic and dualist denials or distortions of nature and history, and on the other isolationist and segregationist denials of human community, young persons are to understand their calling to culture. For schooling this suggests that through books and discussions and careful teaching, young persons be instructed in such matters. Curriculum and learning goals must emphasize that, rather than withdrawal from the world and humankind, the biblical way is openness, concern, and involvement, with all their risks. Comprehensive education like comprehensive religion entails knowing and loving God and our neighbor in the midst of the world.

Our schools will reflect who we, the adult community, are and what we are like. If we show ourselves as fearful and isolationist, content with a kind of ghetto relationship to the wider community around us, so will the school. If the adult community is content with a simple faith and simple morality, proclaimed mainly with otherworldly slogans, so will the school be. If we have no other language for the world around us than the language of creed, cere-mony, or church institutions, frequently pronounced in judgment only, then the schools too will foster such attitudes and goals.

But we can show another face, that of adults who are psycho-logically and socially mature in American society (instead of re-actionary and hostile), a theologically alert and religious community, living out of long and creative theological traditions. If we are culturally oriented Christians, accustomed to speaking in terms of world-and-life view, able to hear and speak to our neigh-bors in the natural discourse of ordinary concerns, and "incarnat-ing" the call to repentance and faith within the fullness of our times, then our schools can be expected to foster the values, goals, and attitudes of such church communities.

Christian education places the child before God and his claims. It is to God above all and to a moral world order that the child in-creasingly must respond. Only as a consequence of this primary re-alignment will the child be able to respond to the other com-plex aspects of the world. A real adjustment to God, to one's fel-low humans and to the world beyond, together with the Christian action that follows, can, in God's providence, produce a Christian culture. And only such a culture, in the last analysis, can bring healing to a society of maladjustment and cynicism, both of which ultimately are spawned by secularism.

There is more to Christian education than testing the spirits; af-firmation comes before the testing and must be its setting and con-text. In that spirit, the daily academic enterprise of teachers and students is a mix of gladly doing the world's work and a growing celebration of what they are coming to see of earth's fullness through the open windows of good subject matter. Like John Cal-vin, who viewed education, farming, and shop keeping as a mix of work and worship, we must see education for the Christian as a sort of daily acknowledgment that "all things" are God's. So, let the school song be not "I am a stranger here" but "this is my Fa-ther's world!"

Christian schools should continue to find their reason for exis-tence not negatively over against failures or weaknesses in public schools, nor for reasons of isolation or separatism, but affirma-tively. No public school can put together the components of true human-religious *transformation* of life and the world; certainly no public school can put together the components of true human-religious *celebration* of life and the world.

In a Christian school young persons must be educated for vital religious response to God from within the fullness of human life. These schools will aim at building a city, the *civitas dei*, where the eyes of all the world may see and know that the integration of reli-gion and culture, rooted in the cultural mandate, is the base-line for constructive Christian living in a pluralistic society. We should not allow the language or the substance of this comprehensive re-ligious vision to fade away. In this tradition lies the strength and the future of Christian education.

CHAPTER SEVEN

Bad Dichotomies

Case Studies in Covenantal Synthesis

Life for persons in the Bible is a complex of rejoicing in the Lord and of finding their way through the tension and diversity of moral decisions in nature and in history.

Those of us in the Reformed tradition seem in a couple of important areas to suffer from something like arrested development, like a troubled young person halfway between the turbulence of adolescence and the composure of adulthood. We are troubled by several disjunctions that blur the Reformed vision and keep us from the maturity we should have attained in both church and education. One might say we are a disjuncting people; our very strength in making distinctions and seeing "the antithesis" tends to make us choose sides where apparent contradictions should not be reduced to one part. We tend to see the alternatives as options to choose between, or even as opposed to each other; we have taken sides, played at winners and losers, looked with suspicion and hostility at each other, and have foreshortened the whole counsel of God in the process. Most grievous of all, we have risked losing the wholeness of the Reformed vision in our educational aims and practices.

But there is a central perspective in the Reformed faith that can help rid us of these dichotomies. The biblical view of covenant can give us direction here, as suggested in previous chapters, for matters both theological and educational. The idea of covenant, which holds God and man in relationship, this world and the other in inseparable tension, shows how we must keep rival claims in balance. We must keep them in balance not only negatively, each canceling out the excesses in the other, but positively, each contributing to the worth of the other, and together reaching a synthesis in which both are given their due. Covenant is a principle of unity requiring two sides kept together, never separated; as such, it can be a model for facing our disjunctions.

I describe here two such disjunctions, the either-or disjunction of piety versus cultural engagement and that of conserving versus reforming. The first asks about our openness to the world, the second about our openness to history. These two major issues were near the surface of the church's thought in the early decades of the twentieth century. They were central not only to Christianity in general but to the life of Christian Reformed churches and to the life of Christian schools, in their thinking and action. Looking back now across a hundred years, it is possible to say that we are still uncertain about these matters. We still find tension between the poles of these dichotomies. I believe a mature faith and loyalty require that we reach some consensus about them in our schools and churches. Exploring them may help us expand our religious vision.

Inward and Outward Commitment

The piety vs. culture question asks whether we are to be private Christians of the heart or public Christians in the world. This old question for Reformed people comes up in classrooms, living rooms, periodicals: should *The Banner* (a publication of the Christian Reformed Church) run film reviews or articles about sexual orientation? how do we read Genesis? what novels can be read in Christian classrooms? do we join in social reform, political action, or environment preservation movements?

May Christians be involved in such "worldly" concerns and programs in ordinary society? Must they not be? What should a Christian choose: private or public Christianity, piety or culture?

It is, of course, a bad question. And many Christians answer it badly, choosing one or the other. For a good answer, Calvinists have two strong (often opposed) traditions to draw on; Calvinists and others should bring them together in a wholeness that can greatly shore up a durable religious vision among us.

83

One tradition is that of the "Afscheiding" Secession mind. The zeal and piety of this tradition characterized many of our forebears among the early Reformed settlers of Iowa, New Jersey, Illinois and Michigan. These Christians could understand Calvin's religion of the burning heart and Augustine's claim that "our hearts are restless until they rest in thee." And though many could not have put it so, their love of the Psalms was a recognition that the covenantal word, in the Old Testament, to "know" the Lord was a word that signified a giving and receiving in a deeply experiential and personal awareness of God.

It had its failings, that 1834 mind. It was narrow at times, and world-denying, self-centered. It was often joyless and fearful, mystical and legalistic, turning young people away. But it had a theological literacy and an existential depth that today's substitutes in crusade exuberance and borrowings from Pentecostal music cannot begin to match. At its best the Secession mind, the piety mind, represented a profound religious depth sustained by faith in Jesus Christ and trust in the promises of God.

Christian schools and churches—from any denomination—will not be strong until we recover some of the best of that personal and experiential religion of the heart. Religious growth needs to be seated deeply in piety.

But what Christian schools and churches need also is the strength of the other root found in Dutch Calvinism, that of the Kuyperian vision of world affirmation. It must be, however, not a second pull on the Christian, but be joined to the other in religious wholeness. To the depth dimension of vital religious relationship must be joined the range and scope of worldly obedience. Kuyper's word that there is nothing in this whole universe of which Christ does not say "this is mine" must again energize our imaginations, our faith, and our world view.

The renaissance in The Netherlands of this second tradition was not accepted all at once—neither in The Netherlands nor in the American Calvinist frontier. Some opposed it out of fear, because it entailed risks; others out of dismay, because it made huge demands on their minds and hearts; others out of dullness and lethargy. But always a core of believers accepted the exhilarating vision and commitment of this approach to life and the world, and gradually in the early decades of this century it took a firm hold on American Calvinist thought and life.

But in recent decades that vision seems to have faded—almost simultaneously with a decline in the experiential aspects of religious life. This invites the speculation that our failure somehow to unite those two roots of our religious life has taken some of the vitality out of each. On the other hand, we have seen among the young in our churches as well as in society all around us a spiritual stirring and a more overt concern for social issues, from human misery to environmental sacrilege. This presents Christian schools and churches a historic opportunity to help invest these revivals of the spirit with the religious depth and durability of world-affirming Calvinism.

I say this not to put down non-Reformed or non-church related activists; we should thank God for them and be humble. I am rather urging that we in the Reformed tradition reaffirm our unique heritage and strength; that we tell our people, show them, especially the young, that they do not need to leave Reformed schools and churches in search for either a warm experiential religion or a public and relevant religion. But then we must believe and demonstrate in education, in church services, and in our way of life that both true piety and cultural obedience are God's will for us; that not one or the other, not the two separately or in tandem, but both together, undivided, is the way of religious wholeness. In our homes and churches and schools we must promote, somehow, a climate of responsible citizenship in the world—not just *next* to piety, not coming after it, but as the other side of it—piety facing outward, engaged up to the hilt with life in all its riches and sorrows.

The Past in the Present

The second bad disjunction we have permitted to develop, contributing also to a sort of identity crisis among us, goes like this: are we to be conserving Christians or reforming Christians? Of course, it might have helped if we had always worded the question this way. When we say "liberal" instead of reforming, the question doesn't get a fair hearing, because liberal is too easily taken to mean politically or theologically liberal. In the form "conserving vs. reforming" the question is more likely to be honestly examined.

But even in this better form, it is a wrong-headed, badly motivated question, which seems to have a life of its own—and should be disposed of. In politics or in religion some people seem to be constitutionally opposed to the notion of conserving, while others are equally automatically opposed to the notion of reforming. The question must be faced if we are to enrich our teaching and preaching and to improve institutional loyalty. Not facing or answering it has blocked intellectual and religious progress in our schools and churches.

Whether we should be a conserving or a reforming people asks about important concerns for thoughtful people that may not be settled in knee-jerk fashion. For example, it involves such matters as liturgical changes or writing new creeds, women in church office or proper Sunday observance, revising report cards or civil liberties for homosexuals, ecclesiastical budgeting for Christian school or how to teach Genesis, new catechism materials or changing the seminary curriculum, political partisanship in schools or choosing novels for English classes. On questions like these it is irresponsible to be unthinkingly either conserving or reforming, at a sort of gut level. To be so alienates; it breeds suspicion, destroys dialogue, corrodes loyalty, and impedes personal growth—and Christian growth is what should mainly characterize Christian churches and schools. Moreover, because these are genuine alternatives, at one time we shall need to be conserving and at another reforming.

Which outlook, which stance, which world view, is the right one? It is a bad question. By this I do not mean that there is no risk here, no paradox, no mystery. The end-time language of the Bible contains warnings, admonitions, challenges that seem to favor the conserving, survivalist stance; it often seems to emphasize only cherishing the traditions and looking to the foundations that have been laid and have stood the test of the ages. On the other hand, there is a progression of God's work in the world, a revelation of his ever fuller word about his relation to the world. The flow of history from Genesis through to the consummation of all things bids all readers of the Bible look up and look forward to the fullness of time, not only to Bethlehem and the cross, but also to the ongoing work and the fullness of time about which Jesus bids us pray when he tells us to pray "your kingdom come on earth as it is in heaven." It is a bad question not because ultimately we believe in a utopian millennium, and do not believe that only darkness and despair lie in human history. It is a bad question because God commands us to be faithful to both sides of this difficult and exhilarating requirement.

So we should resist being either hard-eyed reactionaries or wide-eyed experimentalists, and be instead conservers *and* reformers. As conservers in Calvinist communities and schools we should follow a good instinct to preserve and live out of this virile tradition in theology and history. For us the biblical word "to the law and the prophets" should function not just as a slogan but as a caution within the turmoil and instabilities that contemporary life sets loose each new day. We should be keepers of the altar, guardians of the heritage. The burden of proof should be on the changer.

On the other hand, as Calvinist reformers we should remember that this great tradition was forged no where else than in people's engagement with the life and events of their own times. Such engagement was the church's reforming engagement. In that engagement, the tradition came to life again and again, during the long centuries since the time of the prophets and apostles. It is exactly a tradition of rebels and reformers. The slogan that "a Reformed church is a reforming church" functions as the historical warrant for engaging the world in dialogue and where necessary in confrontation. The reforming tradition sees each new day as a "fullness of time" day in which the offense of the cross continues to turn the world upside down. The reformer rejects subsistence or survival Christianity, and wants to be not just a priestly keeper of the altar but also a living member of the prophetic company celebrated in Hebrews chapter 11.

Should we be conserving or reforming Christians? I believe the most important goal we can set for a durable and portable Christianity in our schools is to aim at being both. Within the Reformed Christian schools, this goal will also move us on toward a self-identity worthy of the tradition, keeping us—or putting us back—into the neo-Calvinism of Abraham Kuyper, the Puritan reforms in England, and the Genevan reformation of John Calvin—and in a proper stance suggested by that Synod one hundred years ago to find our "own reasons" for separate schools.

I believe the Bible supports the quest for such maturity. To know history, the Bible shows, means not that the living are buried in the past but that the dead remain alive in a community of memory. The Bible shows that history is alive, moves on a line, moving toward periodic consummations, but always in a direction and with a momentum that transcend those temporal arrivals and establishments. The movement is always forward and upward. History, as the book of Hebrews marvelously demonstrates, is a quest of the people of God for the city of God.

To nourish and guide this quest in our time, we must recognize that the Bible forbids ignoring a believer's significant choice in history. Choice includes living in tension and in a sort of mania from above, in a holy dissonance. The Bible has both a conserving and a reforming mood. Thus conserving and remembering are enjoined everywhere—enough so to give every true conservative a confirming nudge. It commands parents to teach the things they have learned in the wilderness and in God's words to them throughout their history, to teach these to their children when they sit in their houses and when they walk along the way. When their children ask, what mean these stones? to be able to tell them. The Bible calls on the men and women of God to look to the rock whence they were hewn, to drink from the old wells, to remember that God long ago showed them many things—showed them above all what is good, and what it means to love mercy and to do justly and to walk humbly with their God. Parents are to prod children to ask questions about the tradition, and so hand down the wisdom from the past that will perpetually ensure their hearts and minds.

There is dramatic re-affirmation of the old truth and tradition in the New Testament. Jesus' most scathing rebuke of the religious leaders of his day was that although they sat in Moses' seat, they did not observe what he had commanded; although they multiplied precept upon precept, they had forgotten the weightier matters of the law long ago proclaimed; and most of all, that the reason they did not know him was because they did not know the law and the prophets—did not know the Father long ago revealed to them. The book of Acts, which is Pentecostally wide open to the future, marvelously links that future to the traditions of history and revelation once for all delivered in the Old Testament. It does this in stunning old time historical sermons by Peter and Stephen and Paul. The Bible demonstrates that honoring the old ways and good establishments and, above all, good tradition means not that the living are part of a dead past, are tied to a dead past, but that the dead are vibrantly and instructively alive in the present.

At the same time, the other, the reforming, the changing, is there too. Everywhere in the New Testament we can be reminded, if we look, that the Lord's new day and new times are in reality "the last for which the first was made." We see that the movement, the change, the reforming was in fact the focus of the Bible from the beginning. The biblical word "behold all things are new" is for the end of history, to be sure, but also for the pilgrim church. One-sided conserving Christians should feel ill at ease with the force of this culminating flow of biblical history. The religious reactionary who seldom contributes or celebrates anything new in Christianity should feel ill at ease with the prominence everywhere of innovation, progress, reformation. These are the Bible's themes. The grace of God through Jesus Christ and the redemption of all things, as Colossians puts it, is in the signature of change. The face of the Bible is toward the future, the future of heaven one day, but before that a future of periodic fulfillment in the world and in history. The direction and momentum of biblical religious life are forward. And this the Bible does not let us forget.

Thus Abraham was called out for a life of radical change. There would be for him proximate fulfillment all along the way—in the land of Canaan, and in a chosen nation, but one day in him would all the families of the earth be blessed. Jeremiah announces the end of an age and a new covenant written on the hearts of believers. Isaiah declares that not only Jews but all nations shall come to the holy mountain. Jonah's old-time provincialism was superceded by a stunning gift of grace to pagan Assyria. The Samaritan, despised neighbor to the chosen people, is the hero of the story for all ages, one of our Lord's most dramatic accounts. With another Samaritan, a woman, Jesus flouts convention and discusses theology openly, and announces that neither on the mount where they talked nor in sacred Jerusalem will be the final temple, but in the hearts of believers. Further, Jesus announces revolutionary changes: the outcasts as neighbor; change in Sabbath observance; no, not their expected political Messiah; yes, publicans and harlots and tax collectors too can come in; the wise and the great shall be in the kingdom, but in a miracle and mystery of grace shall first become as little children. Some of the old, says Jesus, is passing, not done away, not all of it, but fulfilled.

Most dramatically of all, with the resurrection of Jesus and Pentecost fifty days later, the flow of change increases. To the disciples on Ascension Day things are still incomprehensible. In this "fullness of time," when the whole future and the whole world beckoned to them to come up further, come up higher, into the kingdom of God, they asked the ultimate establishment question: Lord, will you at this time restore the kingdom to Israel? In his reply, which are his last words on earth, Jesus' three-fold answer speaks to all who are time-bound traditionalists, who are locked into their own place, their own "kind," their own story. No, he says, not only here in Palestine, and not in any other special place, but out into the uttermost parts of the earth. No, he says, not only to the Jewish people, or any other privileged people, but to the strangers among all cultures and peoples out to the uttermost parts of the earth. And no, he says, not today, not in your time, on your calendar, but in God's time, the end of the age. That all this may be, he said, I leave you now to the Spirit whom I will send. He will make of you the rebels and reformers I have called you to be.

But this last word of Jesus does not do it. The preserving, the traditional, the conserving had them locked in. What is needed—for them and for us—is Pentecost. Pentecost is the event and the sign that the church must be open to the future, must move always through time to the drumbeat of God's history. In the advent of the third person of the Trinity the church is given, as Jesus said it would be, a new consciousness. Also, of course, a power (a *dunemos*, as in dynamite), and also a word of witness finally understood. It took that miracle to make followers of Jesus into the reformers he intended them to be. Even so, Peter still needs a roof-top vision, as well as the persuasion of Paul's impassioned argument at the Jerusalem Council. But it came to him, and to the church, and must come to us—what? The radical change in place and people and time of the church's culminating mission out into the world. Peter does accept it, as must all who are open to the miracle of Pentecost and God's history. And it is all such persons, men and women and children, in schools, in homes, and in churches, declares the Epistle to the Hebrews, who must shun the idolatry of their establishments, and who must press on in quest of the heavenly city until the Lord returns. They must go on into the new day of the Lord which, as the Epistle says seven times, is a better way than the old way because it is the way of God's kingdom-coming.

And so it is that Christians today remind themselves that the question, are we to be conserving or reforming Christians, is a wrong question, disallowed by the Bible. The sacred history requires that we be both, all at once. In this way, although we are not of the world, we shall be not of the world *in the midst of the world*. In this way we shall be both open to our times and yet not cut off from the community of memory, the pilgrim company who came before us. We shall celebrate and draw strength from our tradition and heritage, but also move on in the continuing quest, a quest that must either draw us in and catch us up or leave us behind like all those others who were too much at ease in Zion.

Should we be conserving or reforming churches and schools? My proposal is that we must get on with being both—as a kind of habit, a mind set, an instinct. Not forever unsure, but both sides, together, sweating our decisions. Both—not half of each, and not alternately, but joined in a distinctive theology of history.

The Rhythm of Covenant Life

Within each set of disjunctions there is a reciprocal relation, a reversal rhythm. That is to say, the purpose of the piety is to reach outward, have a firm footing for obeying God out in the world. At the same time, the going out and the reaching out in obedience to God in daily life in the world must, as a result of the problems, the struggles, in that reaching out, promote a deeper piety, a greater dependence on God, with the result that there is a mutual strengthening of both.

Similarly for conserving and reforming: the reason we must strike our roots deep and build on the wisdom of the past is so that we may be wise and responsible change agents, wise and responsible reformers, so that we may seek and note God's way as we meet the future. But it is reciprocal. At the same time as we reach out and engage in change, forming change must turn us back each time again to see where we have been, to get strength from the past, to make sure the compass reading is correct. It is a back and forth, an interaction, a reciprocal strengthening that provides the clue and the anchorage to our life in God's world.

Change would in the nature of things be God's way. Institutions have a way of becoming narrow and hard, of becoming establishments. Our schools and churches will resist that only if they are open to the sweep and scope of the Christian mission in the world. That mission requires us to preach and live the whole counsel of God—the vision of a heart of true piety joined to a vibrant affirmation of our cultural calling. Thus we show the power and glory of Christ's kingdom.

In these one hundred years, have those of us in the Reformed tradition made progress in being durable Calvinists with religious faith that is serviceable today? If not, is it because we have grown too comfortable?—too comfortable just because we have forgotten that our concern for orthodoxy, for doctrinal soundness, should all along have had a counterpart of cultural obedience, in which we sought to change things, to transform things, in the name of Christ? Do we have this failure because we have not owned the world of history, culture, and civilization as God's—and therefore ours?

An acceptance of this vision could raise what has so often been mere survival Christianity to something more like triumphal Christianity. It surely could help us know who we are, passing from psychological uncertainty to personal change and maturation. It could form a growing biblical and Reformed consciousness among us.

Vital and productive Christian life and Christian education require careful balancing, fine tuning, between all sorts of apparent opposites. One of the enticements of heaven one day surely is the prospect of putting behind us our present follies, among them our perverse dichotomies and dualisms. Christian education not only prepares for heaven but celebrates, day by day, the present reality of paradise regained, that we are now indeed the children of God.

CHAPTER EIGHT

The Loyal Community

*O Timothy, keep that
which is committed to your trust.*
I Titus 6:20

It needs no pessimist to realize that there is a decline in loyalty to Christian education. We can no longer take for granted that the present generation of young Christian parents will send their children to Christian schools. What can we do about this?

One solution is to rush about concocting superficial adjustments or survival programs: more administrators, more public relations brochures, more "imported" big name speakers—or entertainers, more innovations borrowed from secular journals, and the like. Or we change the curriculum: add more practical courses, opt for values clarification or behavior modification methods, or try Campus Crusade conversion techniques. Though some of this may in the short run be useful, a better solution recognizes that the erosion of loyalty is a crisis of spirit. It means we must probe what is enduring in the religious vision to which we claim allegiance.

But then we must realize that loyalty to Christ does not mean the same thing for all Christians. Their histories differ; they do not just appear. All Christians have a background; they have roots. For Reformed people loyalty to Christ comes shaped and formed by the goodly tradition we have explored. Such loyalty can nurture a rich and exciting kind of education. But if our faith and our institutions are to be durable, our commitment must not be just hanging on to the past, but affirming what in it is good for today. It is the religious vision which must finally distinguish Reformed

Christian schools not only from secular schools but also from fundamentalist Christian schools. Only a renewed vision, integrated with the teacher's skills and competence and devotion, will provide the kind of schooling which deserves our loyalty.

Loyalty to Christ requires that we ask ourselves searching questions: Have we used our cohesive community, our subculture, not as a prop and crutch, but as the custodian of both a great tradition and a great energy for movement—out into the world and forward into history? Have we done all we can, with the same zeal with which we bring programs and buildings into existence, to make the idea behind the slogans and the bricks, the spiritual treasure those programs and buildings represent, precious to our people? Have we used wisely our generous inheritance from the past? Have we in our day added vitality and luster to that tradition, so that the next generation may draw strength and inspiration? The durable Calvinist has staying power, strength of purpose, resilience to present or future shock, and especially has commitment, both at the level of actions and at the level of understanding and moral choice. The durable Calvinist stands in a strong tradition, but is also open—open to new things, to change, to the future, to God, and to God's history.

Calvinist schools are as strong as they are because many teachers, preachers, and ordinary householders are solidly loyal to this tradition. Also present among us, however, are substitute loyalties that we too long have tended to accept as the real thing. One of these is *action* loyalty. It produces good works and keeps things going along pretty well, but because it results either from external pressures or from allegiance to a sub-culture, it could lead to institutional break-down. Of course, you can not have good institutions without loyal acts: regular and generous gifts of time and money, participation in the activities of church or school, retaining membership when the temptation to pull out gets strong—these are indispensable acts of loyalty. Actions, however, are not enough. Action loyalty can be mass produced by all sorts of lower-order motivations: peer or family pressures, fear of other cultures, suspicion of the public school, or even superiority feelings. If the custodians of the community's spiritual health ask for nothing more, if they are satisfied with behaviors of loyalty, the institutions are courting disaster.

To ask about loyalty to the idea of Christian education is to ask about how Christ, through whom all things were created and were redeemed, as Colossians states, is Lord also of education. This first order concern can get us to what is enduring in the Calvinist religious vision. Our community of memory can be the channel for a living tradition and for the energy needed in our time and history. Automatic group loyalties can change to responsible choices.

For the Reformed Christian, loyalty to Jesus Christ is of course a last word, but it is always also a first word for celebrating his present and active lordship. Always much more needs to be said, explained, answered. What, we ask, does loyalty to Jesus mean for believers jointly, collectively, kingdomly? What does it mean culturally, historically? In our answer, we say Christ's kingdom is not just a future kingdom, as many evangelicals say, but is real also today; believers are in that kingdom today. Christ is Lord of history and civilization and education. We have Christian schools not as mission agencies but as academic agencies. We teach the young about God's common grace and special grace, about his special revelation and general revelation. We try to teach the meaning of His Lordship, first, for all of the wide range and complexity of life that a good curriculum presents, and, second, for doing the world's work and living not of the world in the midst of the world. In such education the biblical piety of knowledgeable worship must be bonded to sound learning about God's many-splendored world and about what is evil and what is good in it. First class schools loyal to Christ have a big religious vision.

Loyalty to Christ in Christian education, rooted in the biblical idea of covenant, has two dimensions: that of restricted religion, the piety of the burning heart, love and faith alive in the school; and that of extended religion, preparing the young for obedient life in the world. It means that Christ's word about letting little children come to him be joined to the Old Testament word calling for full time instruction in God's will and ways.

Is it so that we have grown too comfortable, that problems beset us because we have let things drift apart? Have we broken apart our time from God's time, conserving from reforming, piety from culture, theological system from the burning heart, love for our own kind from love for the stranger, loyal actions from loyalty to Christ? If so, such deficiencies in religious wholeness may account for our deficiencies in loyalty to Christian schooling.

Those of us in the Reformed community have a tradition that is both portable and serviceable for our times. Do we stand astride that tradition, leaning against it, drawing wisdom and strength from it, and at the same time prodded by it to face the future with composure and purpose? Are we aware that institutions tend to become establishments, content with middle-age comfort, rooted in the idolatries of place and status; and that just as institutions tend to harden and narrow, so too does loyalty to them? The promotion of true loyalty depends on preventing this narrowing and hardening. Are we alert to the counterfeits of genuine loyalty; do we work at avoiding such by obedience to Christ at those contemporary frontiers and cross-roads where He beckons us follow Him today? Such loyalty to Christ will produce schools that affirm wholeness in the unity and continuity of religion, culture, and education—schools worthy of our whole-hearted loyalty.

PART III

Vision into Practice

CHAPTER NINE

The Religion/Education Analogy

Only as the child of God comes dynamically to know God
(and therefore also humanity and the world and himself)
in God's total revelation and habitually to commit
himself in love to the God he has come to know, will he
be getting the best of God-centered education.

What ought to be clear from the discussion to this point is that the Christian life is a life in relationship; it is the life of a person responding to God's acts, words, gifts, and challenges. More than this, God's encounter of persons is not a complex of static, once-for-all, past-tense occurrences but an ever-continuing reality. For this reason Christian life is described as a life of *faith*, a life of responding, over and over again, to a personal, ever-living God. For this reason, too, Christian life is a life lived in the midst of our times, our world, our society, our fellow believers, our culture—because this is where God has placed us and this is where God seeks us with his acts, words, gifts and challenges. The Christian life is a life of relationship between the believer and God, a relationship not threatened or diminished or distorted by life in the world but fulfilled thereby. The world is the only place a believer has to live the Christian life.

The two poles of that religious relationship between human beings and God are the subjective one that we know as faith and the objective one that we know as God's revelation—these are the ongoing conditions of religious relationship. But now an extremely important clarification must be made, especially in view of the ed-

101

ucational application that may be made of these matters rightly understood. With respect to both faith and revelation, it is possible to have either a partially biblical or a wholly biblical view. Only the latter will serve to enrich not only the Christian life but also the education chosen to serve that life.

With respect to faith, it has already been emphasized that Christian faith is faith in a person; that it includes assent to truths and to Truth, but that at its heart it is commitment, loyalty, service, love, and worship offered to God in Jesus Christ. This view of faith is not an accretion, an addendum, to the idea of faith in the Bible; it is the original and pervasive idea of faith there. The celebrated passages in James 2 on faith and good works; the "applicatory" sections of Paul's letters; the concluding words of our Lord's sermon in Matthew 8 affirming that doers of the Word build on rock and hearers only on sand; the parables of Jesus (especially the Good Samaritan and the Vine and Branches); the judgment announced by John the Baptist; the doom pronounced by the prophets—all are way-stations in the biblical word that faith is the response of a life, not just the acquiescence of a voice, or even the assent of a mind, or the thrill of emotions, or even the routines of prayer, song, and sacrifice. These all point to what God in the original covenant with the man and the woman affirmed to be their part of the relationship: to give themselves to God as God gave and gives himself to humankind.

The New Testament has no good word for the Old Testament word that so richly encompasses this pole of religious relationship. We have to add "and obedience" to the word faith to approximate the real meaning of *faith* (as it is presented, e.g., in Hebrews 11). The Old Testament word is the word *know*. Far from being a mere intellectual and cognitive response, "to know" in the biblical, Semitic sense is to choose, to love, to give oneself to the one who is known. Typical of that meaning are such statements as "You only have I known;" "Adam knew his wife;" "know the heart of the stranger;" "know God and live." This biblical sense of "to know" is to be in relationship to a person, to love that person, to be loyal, to identify with, to give oneself to that person. That also is faith.*

The wholeness of human response in knowing God is possible because persons are indivisible at the depths of their life. To accent this wholeness, another biblical, Semitic word may be paired with such religious knowing; it is the word *heart*. The force of this word, too, should be accepted by New Testament Christians when they consider what is meant by the response of faith. "Keep thy heart with all diligence, for out of it are the issues of life," says Proverbs. Consult a concordance for the rich and varied uses of this word, and it becomes clear that to know in the heart is the only kind of response that can satisfy the first great condition of religious relationship, the condition we have called faith.

Education that seeks only a response of verbal affirmation, of understanding in the mind, of knowledge that certain things are the case will fail to be good Christian education. We shall argue later that intellectual or rational growth is indispensable to Christian education and to Christian living, but that this is so only if and when other learnings are intimately conjoined with the intellectual. An analogy exists between the whole response of religious faith, seated in the heart (that is, at the depths of personal existence), and the sort of whole learning that ought to result in a school; for learning too is a kind of Semitic knowing, a response of understanding, of acceptance, of commitment to what is learned. If less than this, it is incomplete learning and useless; unless it is completed it will wither away. The activity of faith and the activity of learning are in many respects similar. Subjective reaching out in vital concern is indispensable to real learning and to true faith. Both are response at the depths of the person's life and in the whole of that life. This reaching out in whole response is, however, only half the story of either religious or educational relationship. The circuit must be closed; in fact, prior provision for the possibility of a circuit must exist. That is to say, a response takes place against a prior stimulus, in this case a prior engagement or encounter.

---

* For more detailed discussion of the words *know* and *heart,* see Chapter Four.

For religious relationship, this prior condition is the objective reality of God's word to humankind, his revelation; for the educational process it is the objective givens of what we call curriculum. Objective revelation evokes, elicits, draws forth a person's subjective knowing of God, as faith. Objective curriculum draws forth the child's subjective knowing of life and the world, as vital learning. In both cases a suitable tension and accommodation is reached between a disciplining objective given and a vital subjective response. In both cases a circuit is closed.

This is again to suggest that, as with learning and believing, the functions of curriculum and the functions of revelation are in many respects similar. In each case an objective referent comes to bear, in the one case upon the student seeking to learn in school, and, in the other, upon the sinner seeking fulfillment in a life with God. In the case of either curriculum or revelation, the authority and validation with which it supports its claim to present most urgent matters are indispensable, to significant educational engagement on the one hand, and, on the other, to significant religious engagement. Both claim to encounter their object at the depths of and in all parts of personal life.

The further point may now also be made that just as the objective requirement of revelation and the subjective requirement of faith are both essential, in their vital interrelationship, so, in a similar vital interrelationship, both curriculum and the learning process must each be given its due. Neither religious relationship nor educational relationship is fulfilled unless the circuit between their two parts has been closed.

Of course there are vast differences between Christian faith and the ordinary learning process. And it should at once be clarified that in only one sense, beyond that of formal analogy, are revelation and curriculum spoken of in the same breath. Unlike revelation, which is God-given and comes with its unique perfections and authority, curriculum construction is subject to gross and pervasive error. Curriculum's chief mark should be its openness to correction, improvement, or abandonment. Moreover, there is more in a school that comes with claims and authority than curriculum.

Yet there is one sense in which I do wish to press a connection between revelation and curriculum. When all due allowance has been made for the open, fallible, imperfect construct we call curriculum, it remains true that curriculum for Christians brings together in a pattern those things which they believe a) are most in accord with the way things are or ought to be and b) are teachable to the group for whom it is constructed. Holding to a realistic view of knowledge, a Christian wants to know and teach about things that are given, that are discoverable, that are pointers to what is the case—in the world, in nature, in society, in the human heart, in history. Desiring also to teach what ought to be, what can be done, how things should go, why things are or are not so; desiring above all to move students to some kind of action, purpose, or quest, the teacher or school puts together for this or that grade, its construct of truth, of revelation, of objectively knowable things (facts, meanings, values, understanding, skills). More than this, teachers claim that this is (for now) the best of all possible constructs. They assign authority to it, and seek to validate all of it in whatever way they can.

In that sense Christian teachers cannot escape the notion that here, in curriculum construction, they are busy with revelation, be it only an emerging reflection of the other revelation. They not only speak of general revelation, as this doctrine is held in Reformed theology, but dare even to say: as of now, this is God's word as I see it; help me, God, to use it wisely and competently for the Christian growth of Christian students. And in that same sense, of course, the learning process in a Christian school comes close, for all its difference, to the process of believing itself. It will be not a believing in subject matter, of course, not even in the clearest truths of subject matter. Nor will it be mainly a believing that God wants us to learn this or that and then learning it. It will be a believing which is the other side of living, a believing as a response, as a self-giving—to learning, not only, but to the life that curriculum is helping students to understand, commit themselves to, and participate actively in. Something of the intent of this analogy ought to inform our idea of curriculum. If the student is to respond in learning at the depths of life, first in order that it may truly be learning, and second in order that it may become an experience in the Christian response of faith itself, then the choice of curriculum and of what we do in the various subjects ought to be a more awesome and careful undertaking than it sometimes is.

Finally, just as the biblical idea of faith is a far richer idea than we often let it be, so it should now be stressed that the biblical idea of revelation is a far richer idea than we often let it be. Much of the foregoing suggested that revelation is not the static, cut-off, Bible-encased set of verbal symbols we often reduce it to. Of course, the Bible is God's word; of course, no further miraculous revelations are publicly possessed; and without this Book there would be no record of God's revelation. But there is more than all this to revelation—more even to the Bible. The Bible is a living, breathing, speaking, acting reality; that is, the Bible used by God today is all of that. This we must be receptive to if we want to capture the meaning of religion as relationship, of faith as faith in a person, and of Christian education as education for a life of Christian response to a living God who meets us in the midst of the twentieth century world—the world of work and play, of struggle, of anxiety; the world of nature and culture; the world of church and home and education. Here God meets us or pursues us or drives us. Here we must respond, respond to living disclosures and encounters of the living God.

Therefore, without denying that we are Bible-bound in a very real way, we must nevertheless see that the Bible is not bound. One way to understand how it can be that even the Bible-bound believer ought to be caught up in the reality of on-going dynamic contemporaneous revelation is to consider how the idea of revelation functioned in biblical, especially Old Testament, times. As with the concept of faith as knowing God, so it is with the concept of God's speaking to human beings. To limit faith to an intellectual response of assent or acquiescence is almost to miss the heart of it. So to limit revelation to intellectual and verbal communications is almost to miss all of it. To understand revelation we must understand it, says the Calvinist theologian Gerhardus Vos, as a noun of action.

As more clearly seen in the Old Testament, although certainly not missing in the New, revelation is the counterpart of knowing in the Semitic sense, of responding as a changed person. Revelation always changes a person: it reaches the person at the depths of life. It is creative, generative, even in those who reject God. They never are unchanged—as can easily be the case if revelation is only verbal, cognitive, or discursive. There is creative, encountering force to what God does when he speaks. Both creation and redemption are by God's word made incarnate in two unique ways. The creation of the world is variously described as a commanding, as a calling forth, as making with the "breath of his mouth," as a "framing" by the word of God. God's word, written or spoken, is described as life-giving, life sustaining. So redemption is begun with the word becoming flesh; spiritual life is begotten through the word; it is kept alive by the word. The miracle of Pentecost and the Tongues is the guarantee that the new life will be transmitted to the world by a word of birth, of power, of fulfillment. And Christ, who rides to victory in the great consummation, with a word in his mouth, seated on a white horse, is again called the Word of God.

The word of revelation, according to the Bible, is a word of creativity and of power, intended to move and change the receiver. It is the coming into relationship of the One in whom act and word are one. Little wonder, then, that the only adequate response today or at any time of persons to this encountering, speaking God is to go beyond mere words or acquiescence to response with their entire being. For in the great biblical metaphor of covenant this is what God himself does when he initiates relationship, and such response alone can complete relationship.

Something like this idea of God's continuing speech to humankind, made more eloquent, more unique, more compassionate, and more urgent in Jesus Christ and in the continuing miracle of Pentecost, ought to inform our conception of the Christian life, and therefore our conception of the education we give in preparation for that life.

CHAPTER TEN

Educational Applications
of Biblical Religion

In the real world of the Christian school
nothing is more important than getting clear
on the religious vision of Christian education,
and then letting that vision control the aims
and practices of teachers in the classroom.

For religion to function as a direct and substantial control on a school's goals, curriculum, and method, it is necessary to identify the essential religious principles relevant to education as well as draw out their implications. In this chapter I will summarize the discussion of the biblical foundations (the materials presented in Chapter Four) as such principles or criteria and offer their educational applications. These applications are presented, however, not as necessarily implied in each case, but rather as reasonable educational extensions of comprehensive covenant religion.

The Scope and Quality of Biblical Religion

Major biblical criteria include:

1) religion, as a covenantal relationship of ultimate concern, is both objectively and subjectively comprehensive;

2) its objective comprehensiveness is established in God's revelation in the Bible and in all of reality as it encounters human beings;

3) its subjective comprehensiveness is established in human-kind's endowment for knowing God in the Semitic sense and in human calling to religious response in all of life;

4) creation in the perspective of Christ's redemption and redemption in the perspective of creation define the conditions of human physical-spiritual existence.

Extensive educational applications are drawn from these criteria:

First. Parents and community should rear the young in comprehensive religious understanding and commitment, emphasizing the following:

a) that Christianity, being neither otherworldly nor part-time, rejects all spiritual-physical dualisms;

b) that although religion has indispensable ceremonial, creedal, and institutional expressions, it is far more than these; it is also a world and life view; and

c) that the education of children and young people in such comprehensive religion is not optional or an addendum in Christianity but is itself an obligation in covenant stewardship.

Second. The comprehensive nature of such education is determined not primarily in the grace and gospel mandate of Matthew but in the culture and history mandate of Genesis. The gospel, the covenant of grace, and parental baptism vows are of great importance to Christian education, especially regarding the urgency of such education, but for its aim, curriculum, and processes the creation perspective is indispensable.

Third. In a division of labor, when the school is assigned the role of formal education (in the assumption that home and church are carrying out their roles in Christian nurture), the school will be centrally concerned with the natural, human, cultural, and "worldly" aspects of comprehensive religion. Its curriculum and its learning goals will be directed, respectively, toward setting forth a religious view of all of life and toward the pupil's acceptance of such a view in personal commitment.

Fourth. In the school's dual concern with curriculum and learn-ing, the analogy of revelation and knowing as the two conditions of covenant relationship should guide the school, first, because the pupil's learning is to be a comprehensive *knowing*, as re-sponse; and second, because a schools curriculum is to be a com-prehensive *revelation* by which the response is elicited. In Christian education, with its emphasis upon special revelation and a growing religious relationship, this analogy is a suitable one. For while human curriculum theory and pattern are fallible and subject to gross error, the school's purpose with curriculum is to elicit by means of it a suitable learning response. A Christian ap-proach to learning requires a Christian approach to curriculum first of all.

Fifth. Christian education will therefore emphasize, on the one hand, the curricular importance of the objective realities of nature, culture, and history—and of God's revelation in relation to these; and, on the other hand, the importance of subjective response to those realities; but it will emphasize that such a response is to be by the whole person in ultimate concern and commitment, and not a mere cognitive or verbal response.

The Importance of the Natural

Major biblical perspectives on nature, culture, and stewardship include the following:

1) nature in all its forms, including the physical, cultural, and human conditions of life, is God's covenantal gift to humankind;

2) the restoration of all things by Christ applies to the realities of nature, of culture, and of human relationships and institutions; it restores human physical-spiritual wholeness and reaffirms the Genesis mandate; and

3) human beings, created to be both within and above nature, are called to a religious stewardship which includes understand-ing, appreciation, use, and enlargement of the gifts of nature and the offering of this cultural activity in religious service to God.

On the basis of these criteria we may draw many educational applications.

First. The Christian school will show and teach the following as a major emphasis in its educational philosophy:

· a) that the natural dimensions of life (the human body, the earth's treasures, the cultural deposit, the organization of social life, the depth and variety of interpersonal relationships) are God's gifts to us, are therefore good and not evil, are not in opposition to the "spiritual;" they are not to be merely tolerated as lower than spiritual, nor exploited for either spiritual or secular reasons, but are to be prized and honored for their intrinsic worth;

b) that nevertheless they are created and not ultimate; as withdrawal in asceticism or dualism is wrong so too the worship of nature and culture in humanism and secularism is wrong; and

c) this means that humankind is called to hallow the human, the natural, and the cultural realities of life; that we are to transcend nature not by fleeing or denying it but by using and dedicating it according to divine norms.

Second. Because the prizing of the natural, the cultural, and the human begins with understanding them, a Christian school will

a) prominently emphasize the natural and social sciences, literature and the arts, and related curriculum components;

b) require of the pupils a mastery of the skills necessary to such understanding and practice of the habits of reading and thinking appropriate to the subject areas; and

c) emphasize that significance and meaning depend not on the utility of curriculum areas but on the objective truth and value which have their source in God.

Third. Beyond such cognitive learning in its emphasis on stewardship in the natural and cultural domains, the school will also promote the moral and creative growth for which those subjects offer continuing opportunity. All should be focused for religious development and response to God.

Fourth. Further, a Christian school will emphasize that stewardship in the natural and cultural includes also their enlargement and extension as human work in the world. Students will be taught that not only the contemplation, re-ordering, or enjoyment of nature and culture but reconstruction and new creations are the goals of Christian stewardship.

Fifth. Because success in the foregoing depends on whole *response,* that is, on true learning, on understanding, acceptance, and commitment by the learner, the school will strive

a) to relate learning to familiar knowledge and relationships already learned;

b) to take account of the physical and psychological developmental needs and conditions of the learner;

c) to ensure that self-knowledge and personal freedom with respect to the natural and human conditions of life become part of the learner's growth; and

d) to regard such growth of young Christians as indispensable to their emerging religious response to God.

The Challenge of History and Community

From our discussion of these biblical perspectives, we draw the following criteria:

1) God's sovereignty in nature and in grace directs human history to the coming of Christ's kingdom;

2) human beings have the dual obligation to acknowledge this sovereignty and at the same time to grow as unique individuals through significant historical, that is, irrevocable, moral choices;

3) order and freedom so related are the ultimate religious conditions of human historical life within nature and society;

4) faith in Christ and covenant obedience to God require not escape from but acceptance of the complexities and moral tensions of historical and communal life and response to them in personal freedom and choice.

**In consideration of these criteria,
we elicit the following educational applications.**

First. The school should emphasize the following with respect to the student's understanding and acceptance of his place in history:

a) that in the rich variety of his natural and human existence (as set forth previously) he must try to discover God's way and will and purpose in history and thereupon direct his life in harmony with that purpose in significant moral choices;

b) that in all of his natural, cultural, and human relationships he is to be loyal, creative, and neighborly;

c) but that in all of these relationships, which at times become restrictive or tempt him to conformity and security, he is to live as individual person, ultimately loyal to God and therefore also to himself in his relationship to God;

d) that the student's ultimate commitment to God requires that, in reverence and love, he seek first the kingdom of God, that is, accept God's will for history as the supreme law of his life; and

e) that such religious life in history is not simple or clearly marked out but entails moral tension and conflict, and therefore requires decisive choice and act.

Second. Specifically, the Christian school should emphasize and demonstrate the following with respect to *society* (as a given group, religious or secular, in a given time and place) and *history* (as the movement toward universal community of which the kingdom of God is the heart):

a) that a Christian lives in both at once and that understanding of the conditions and needs of both is of great importance;

b) that the demands of both are sometimes irreconcilable, the one pulling toward security, conformity, and group identity, the other compelling toward uniqueness, decision, self-acceptance, and obedience to God;

c) that it is in moral tension between the rival claims of society and history in this sense that persons live and must find their way;

d) that the way cannot be found by denying the claims of either, that only in a time and place can the Christian live for a purpose beyond time and place; and

e) that understanding and acceptance by the students of these conditions of human life, and of their need to live morally within those conditions, is an important goal of Christian education.

Third. The Christian school should illustrate the above matters, and bring the student to understanding and personal growth in them, by means of a variety of learning experiences, but mainly and continuously by means of the rational-moral disciplines of curriculum, as follows:

a) religious studies should provide synoptic estimates and summaries of the kinds of moral-religious issues which are part of life, as well as standards by which choice and decision may be guided;

b) studies in literature (beyond the pleasure they afford) are of unsurpassed value in revealing moral conflict and tension. Depicting persons in their failure to choose, in wrong choices and in right choices, a study of good literature presents concrete embodiments of significant human life, and is indispensable to Christian education;

c) studies in history are equally indispensable for revealing models of uniqueness in human decision and act; for emphasizing the permanent and unrepeatable character of such acts, and for providing clues to new contexts and conditions which repeatedly challenge persons to unique choice and act.

Fourth. In its emphasis on responsible moral choice, Christian education will

a) relate such choice directly to the student's commitment to Jesus Christ, in faith and love;

b) further relate such choice to the complexities of comprehensive religion as a covenant with God in all of life;

c) take the students far beyond mere verbal learning to the point where, in a biblical sense of knowing, they respond in a whole commitment, immediately to the education they are receiving and ultimately to the goals of the kingdom of God.

Human Nature and Calling

**The biblical perspectives on this subject
yield the following criteria:**

1) human nature and needs are to be defined and understood
a) by the physical-psychological-spiritual realities of their humanity;
b) by their unique rational, moral, and creative endowments in a personal wholeness, as created in the image of God; and
c) by their religious calling to covenantal response in special attitudes and acts of worship and in stewardly work within the world;

2) in the restoration of all things by Christ, human calling, personal wholeness, and the essential endowments for the fulfillment of calling were all restored.

**All that we can learn about human beings from the Bible
and from the sciences which our biblical position warrant
leads to educational applications such as follow.**

First. Because the student is called to comprehensive religious response, the Christian school will emphasize both curriculum and the learning process:
a) it will emphasize objective *curriculum* which, despite its fallible, changing, and open character, is nevertheless analogous to revelation in religion; the goals and disciplines of curriculum are the school's recognition of the objectively real world of nature and history, and of the prior reality of God as creator; curriculum is the school's commitment to a realistic view of human knowledge;
b) at the same time the school will emphasize subjective *learning* and human development as analogous to knowing in the biblical sense; the concern of the school for such heart-knowledge constitutes its recognition that human nature is a unity, and that significant human response is indivisible;
c) moreover, the school will emphasize both at the same time, holding that neither subject matter without vital response nor

whole-life learning without the rigors of curriculum pattern and content is real education. Objective curriculum must psychologically and developmentally encounter the student, and subjective learning must be a response to the range, variety, and complexity of good curriculum.

Second. The school will take account of the physical-psychological as well as the spiritual-religious needs of the pupil, especially as these relate to his rational, moral, and creative functions:

a) the physical-psychological needs will be met by means of the best procedures and methods that the science of teaching and the data of physiology, psychology, and sociology require;

b) the spiritual-religious needs will be met by means of the integration of religion in the school with religious nurture in the home and church; by means of special religious studies in the school; and by means of direct challenges to the pupil to commit his whole life to God in Jesus Christ, particularly as the school's curriculum is helping him to see the expanded scope of that commitment.

Third. The school will mainly focus on the rational, moral, and creative functions and endowments of the student; they are the doorway through which curriculum comes to the student and through which the student responds to the curriculum; through these functions he achieves comprehensive *knowing*.

Fourth. Thus the school will define the pupil's educational need, not in terms first of all of his nature, physical or spiritual, but in terms of his endowments as they relate to his calling. In meeting that need the school helps the pupil to grow in his physical-spiritual nature, to learn about his vocation in the world as image of God, and to mature in obedience to that vocation.

CHAPTER ELEVEN

The Two Sides of
Christian Education

Education is a journey.
If we are to go in the right direction
we need a clear philosophy of education.
Then it might be a good trip.

How can the comprehensive religious vision for Christian education become more than a preamble? How must that vision come to control decision-making in a school's educational program? The difficulties and hazards of making this connection doubtless explain why only rarely in the past attempts to do so were made, and why, when they were made, they left most teachers and parents confused or unconvinced. Despite the risks, if the terms *Christian* and *education* are in fact to enrich each other and if the worth of Christian education depends, finally, on that interrelation and mutual enrichment, the task of bringing religious presuppositions to bear on the educational program must be undertaken.

In which areas of a school's program should those presuppositions come to bear directly and strategically? It will be argued here that they should be the two areas of *learning goals* and *curriculum pattern*. That is to say, after the school has asked and answered the religious question, it should ask, *first:* What sorts of growth, what changed abilities, performances, behavior, insights, attitudes, values, dispositions should the school emphasize as most appropriate to its religious vision? and, *second:* What curriculum pattern, what subject matter, what areas of study, should a school emphasize as most appropriate to its religious vision and to those learning goals? A school may err in choosing its learning goals and its curriculum priorities and should therefore remain open to new insights; but given its claim to have an educationally relevant religious commitment, it cannot avoid these questions. They have to do with the basic strategies of a Christian school.

Education as Vital Learning and Disciplining Curriculum

Christian educators ought not to let these two questions be wrenched apart. Almost from the beginning of modern schooling, in what has come to be the great debate in education, teachers have tended to choose between them, to emphasize either the objective side of education (the content of curriculum) or the subjective side (the changing person). Whether arising in the soil of philosophical systems or in the practice of perceptive teachers who sought to counteract trends they judged to be miseducative, this polarization has often led to a short-circuiting of genuine education. The great debate comes to its baldest expression when so-called curriculum-oriented teachers callously consign all but the highest IQ students to a sort of educational wasteland and when so-called learning-oriented teachers solemnly intone the syntactical and educational nonsense that they teach pupils, not subject matter. Christian educators should avoid such educational dichotomy.

Christian educators should also go beyond the more responsible versions of the great debate that have illumined and enriched past discussions of Christian education, most notably in the writings of W. H. Jellema and C. Jaarsma.[*] Accepting their fair-sighted and durable contributions and disregarding at this point the rather basic differences between them, especially regarding the school's comprehensive religious vision, teachers in

---

[*] For example, see Jellema in *The Curriculum in a Liberal Arts College* (Calvin College Monograph, 1958), and "Calvinism and Higher Education" in *God-Centered Living* (Baker, 1951). See also Jaarsma in *Fundamentals in Christian Education* (Eerdmans, 1953), and *Human Development, Learning, and Teaching* (Eerdmans, 1959).

Christian schools should seek to direct the contributions of these men into the advancement of contemporary Christian education.

Thus teachers should accept as sound doctrine Jaarsma's major thesis about education as *response:* that education will fail unless it is suited to the learner, to his previous learnings, to his emerging self-awareness; that nothing is learned, educationally or religiously, until it is learned in the *heart,* until it is understood, appropriated, and responded to deep down where a person lives; and that even the best of curriculum will be unrewarding and oppressive unless the learner's response to it is vital and cumulative in the ongoing *process* of personal growth.

But teachers should also accept Jellema's major thesis about education as *encounter:* that the right things, the most educationally rewarding things—the things that a school as *school* must teach about the wholeness of life and truth—must be studied. W.H. Jellema taught that as all education is by and for a kingdom, demanding ultimate allegiance, so Christian education must serve the *city of God;* and that even the best of both method and aim will be short-circuited unless they are joined to a *required* curriculum whose well-taught content disciplines young Christians for living the full-orbed Christian life.

Of course, in theory almost no one deliberately separates these two sides of education. In practice, however, the difficulty of keeping learner and subject matter in range of each other and the failure to make programmatic provision for such interaction lie at the center of the age-old educational debate.

Christian schools must go beyond taking sides in this debate. They should accept the best of the learning-oriented approach and the best of the curriculum-oriented approach and refocus them for the sort of educational closure required by a Christian vision of human calling and of human endowments. The Christian school's model should be not the reductions born of teacher preferences or philosophical systems but the Bible's view of God and his image-bearers in relationship. Similar to the way closure in religious growth requires both God's disciplining encounter of persons through his Word and world and a vital human response to that en-

119

counter in the biblical sense of knowing (as including also loving and serving God), so it is in educational growth: the objective and the subjective are alike indispensable. For both religious and educational reasons, Christian schools should keep the two sides of education together.

If the commitment to keep them together is made, subject matter will find its place in the school as the indispensable *means* to human growth in education. Fallible and liable to error as a curriculum structure may be, in a Christian school it nevertheless aims to come with a unique authority, the authority of objective truth and reality. On the other hand, authoritative as a curriculum may be, it remains a means, a means to nothing else than evoking the young person's response in vital educational growth. A school's curriculum must be organized for learning, and a young person's learning must be in response to curriculum. It is through the two together, not through either alone, nor through both separately or alternately, that a school must aim at educational closure.

If this commitment is made, the teacher will above all aim at personal development and growth in young persons. To achieve this, pupils must be interested, motivated, involved; they must be active in the educative process. They must be moved and must be in motion. They must grow. They must *learn.* But the teacher will remember that this change and growth must be in response to something. To what? To what the teacher brings. The teacher is there: she arouses the pupil, engages and stimulates learning. How is this done? It is done with curriculum.

It is not just anything at all that the young person in a schoolroom must be vitally active about; the schoolroom is not the playground, the school bus, the family dinner table. It is the schoolroom. This is where the teacher brings new, significant, disciplining experiences into the lives of young Christians. A wise teacher will, of course, all along the way promote schoolroom learning by means of all sorts of out-of-school experiences. But even these must be reconstructed and expanded in the schoolroom, so that new experience enriches and expands familiar experience. Because new experience is imported and introduced, it must be carefully planned, measured, and organized by the teacher. The experience must elicit *responses* within learners to what for them are new encounters with the world of nature, society, culture, history, and, above all, with God—to whom all of it must be related. To such encounters with all sorts of things that normally do not come up in ordinary experience, the learner must be guided by the teacher.

Relating such new experiences conceptually to the pupil's ordinary experience, previous learnings, and expanding awareness and concerns, the teacher aims at the *enlargement* of the pupil's life. These new experiences may include the geography of China, the music of Gershwin, the processing of milk, the politics of the Civil War, the poems of Keats, the ideology of the New Left. They may include studying the crusades, painting in water colors, experimenting with air pressure, comparing sixteenth century plays, analyzing race relations, memorizing Psalms. They include whole blocks of matters that do not come up on a playground or in ordinary life. The teacher sees to it that they come up in a school, in its curriculum.

It is as response to the fulness and excitement of *curriculum* that the wise teacher promotes the interest, participation, discovery, and freedom that constitute learning. And it is to encounter the students—their capacities, experience, readiness, and needs— that the wise teacher organizes, shapes, and introduces curriculum. One concern without the other would lead to far less than half of good education. When the necessary *interaction* between subjective learning and objective curriculum has been accepted by a teacher as the nonnegotiable condition of educational growth, then the next questions may be asked: What should be the major learning goals and what should be the preferred curriculum pattern of a Christian school?

Selecting Major Learning Goals

Of the almost limitless kinds of learning a Christian school could promote, which should it mainly aim at? This question should be distinguished from the question that asks about the intricacies of the learning *process;* those intricacies are many and require careful analyses and prescriptions in a philosophy of the teaching-learning process. What the present question asks about is the important intermediate step between a school's religious vision and the teaching-learning process, a step that needs more prominent attention than it often receives. This question asks about the *changes* in young persons that a school's teaching-learning process ought mainly to aim for.

Which kinds of changes, of learning growth, should these be? They should be the kinds that most directly take account of the learner's nature and needs. In the Christian perspective that nature and those needs are to be determined in two ways: *empirically,* by carefully studying human persons in their life situations, but also *theologically,* by asking about the religious calling and endowments of human persons. Understood in both these ways, the nature and needs of students require above all their *educational* growth as a knowing, choosing, and acting persons. From within their personal, worldly existence and in response to the wide range and variety of life that a curriculum introduces them to, young person must progressively grow in the competence and disposition to *understand* the Christian life, to *choose* the Christian life, and to *live* the Christian life. If by Christian life is meant the full-orbed life of covenantal obedience, such growth is indispensable.

These three kinds of learning growth correspond formally to what many modern educators are again distinguishing as cognitive, affective, and activity growth. They are here designated intellectual, moral, and creative growth. Remembering that boundaries cannot really be set between them and that in any case the growth of young persons takes place in all these ways interrelatedly, Christian teachers should nevertheless mark such growth off for distinguishable learning goals—for unit studies, for semester courses of study, and for the overall program of the school.

Intellectual growth. Acceptance by teachers of these learning goals means that they should constantly ask how they can help young persons understand things as they are; how they can foster in the learners a growing insight into the natural, social, cultural, historical, and religious conditions of human existence—within whose complexities and opportunities they must seek out the truth about things and live the Christian life. Teachers should recognize that for such growth young persons need intellectual education through suitable curriculum.

Moral growth. Teachers should also ask how they can guide young persons by means of their growing understanding of life and the world toward a deeper *commitment* to the way things ought to be, to the true and the good; how they can promote increased sensitivity to, and more careful discrimination between, right and wrong, particularly as the learners are coming to understand the complexities of moral life in the world; how, through the students' expanding awareness of the moral options that life presents, teachers can guide them to choose Christian options, based on Christian commitment. Teachers should recognize that for such growth young persons need *moral* education through suitable curriculum.

Creative growth. Teachers should also ask how they can help free young persons from fear or inertia through growth in self-acceptance and self-expression; how they can help them grow from an inward beholding of the truth and an inward commitment to the good toward a disposition to *participate* in life; how they can guide the growing understanding and commitment of young persons toward both a unique personal life and a loyal life within human community; how they can guide young persons to express both their freedom and their obedience in a productive Christian life. Teachers should recognize that for the nurture of such dispositions and self-expression they must provide education for creative growth through suitable curriculum.

Selecting Curriculum Priorities

Of the almost limitless sorts of subject matter a school could teach, which should be its priority subject matter? Apart from its electives, which should be its *core* subjects required of all normal young persons? This question must be distinguished from questions about graded *courses of study*. The latter, having to do with grouping, fusing, and integrating subject areas for suitable teaching and learning, certainly need close and careful attention. But the present question asks about a prior matter. It asks about major areas or patterns of subject matter; it asks about the school's curriculum *commitment*—something that must be settled before course of study writing can proceed.

Which curriculum areas should a Christian school mainly emphasize? It is held here that they should be those, first, that most directly and suitably promote the sorts of learning growth discussed above and, second, that most directly take account of the wide range and variety of the world in which God has placed human beings. This is to say that religious growth and therefore learning growth should be in *response* to curriculum encounters that present the wholeness of life and reality—the wholeness presented in the physical world, in human society, in human culture, in the continuity of history—all of it in its relationship to God.

Although names given to major curriculum areas will vary with different educators, what is proposed here is that on levels of complexity suitably adjusted to the readiness of the learner and in courses of study suitably organized for various grade levels, a Christian school's required core curriculum should prominently include the following groups of studies.

General Development Studies. These studies, concurrent with and important to all the others, must meet the students' developmental needs as responders to their education. Such studies include the all-important verbal and mathematical masteries of the three R's, but also, as part of the same class of basic learnings, continuing studies in music, art, speech, writing, and physical education. These all are developmental in the sense that each promotes, in its own way, the sorts of responses and dispositions that are indispensable to the learner's self-acceptance and participation—in the learning process and in ordinary life outside school.

Natural Sciences and Mathematics These studies present human physicalness as well as the natural environment. Through mathematical understanding and through the disciplines of scientific method, these studies should prepare young persons to know and respond to the laws and processes, but also to the gifts and splendors of their physical existence. Through these studies the school must challenge the learner to understand, to appreciate, to use, and to extend the treasures of nature—in harmony with its ways, in service to others, and in stewardship to God.

Social Sciences. In these studies, societal life and environment in all their diversity and complexity are examined. They present human needs and tensions in the many relationships, organizations, and institutions, all understood as our *shared* life within ordinary society. These studies challenge the young person, through both empirical observations and moral judgments, to understand, appreciate, and participate in human interrelations within society—in appreciation of our human family and in obedience to God.

History Studies. These studies present our historical existence. They present human beings, who live in nature and society, as living also in a vertical environment, in a chain of relationships that not only unites past, present, and future, but also discloses meanings and understandings essential to knowing contemporary life. Through imaginative reconstruction of the past by means of appropriate historical inquiry, these studies emphasize that individuals live inescapably within a flow of time, but also within once-for-all situations in which goals must be set and decisions made. Presenting failures and tragedies as well as successes and achievements, history studies must make clear to young persons that of them, too, are required unrepeatable personal choices within the structures of nature and society, but also within a flow of time that requires openness to God's purposes both in and beyond history.

Literature and the Arts. The studies in this group present human creative perceptions and responses within nature, society, and history. Through a wide variety of artistic and literary forms, they present human beings as fashioners and sharers of an inner vision. In addition to the knowledge, pleasure, and appreciations these studies foster, literature and the arts can help young persons to prize their own personal identity and that of others, to find and love their neighbors in authentic human relationships, and in these ways also to discover how truth and compassion revealed in the manner appropriate to art can enrich their religious growth.

Religious Studies. In these studies God's special revelation to humankind is presented. Centering in the redemptive love of Jesus Christ, they present us as engaged by God and as commanded to respond to God from within our natural, social, historical lives—to respond, moreover, as both unique persons and as contributing members of the Christian community. The perspective of these studies enriches and illumines all other studies, and with special directness challenges young persons to know and hear and respond to God from within the fulness of their own expanding life and world.

* * * * *

Of course, the various dimensions of life and the world distinguished in these curriculum groups do not represent separate domains of human existence; they are all interrelated, and in a Christian school especially, our relation to God will be stressed in all studies. But these groups of studies do present *conceptually* distinguishable areas of life and the world, and also distinguishable modes of inquiry by which life and the world may be known. Such a conceptual cataloguing of both content and modes of inquiry can alert teachers, when they fuse or integrate various studies—history and social studies, say, or literature and reading—not to obscure the essential content or discipline of any of the combined studies. Regardless of how subject matter is rearranged for teaching and learning, the school ought to let curriculum groupings like those above function as reminders of what curriculum ought to do and be in Christian education and function also, therefore, as a prod and a guide in the school's periodic self-examination.

If a Christian school seeks by means of both its major learning goals and its priority curriculum commitments to bring about whole education—whole with respect to the learner's intellectual, moral, and creative endowments and whole with respect to the range and complexity of the world around each child, and if such educational fulfillment is shaped by the school's religious aim, the result could be superior Christian education.

CHAPTER TWELVE

Notes on the Teaching/Learning Spectrum

It is in the heart, it is the way God's word
must be put in the children's hearts,
that lies at the core of Christian education.

Note: The following addenda expand on subjects introduced in previous chapters.

Educational Closure

Success in an educational articulation of comprehensive religion depends on closing the circuit between good curriculum and teaching on the one hand and genuine learning and commitment on the other. Both are necessary in a continuum, somewhat as revelation and knowing in the biblical sense are both necessary for their completion in genuine relationship. In this way covenant is a model for closure in education.

The key to holding the objective and subjective sides of education together lies in correctly defining the student's religious and educational need. That need, according to the Bible, is defined in terms of human endowments as rational, moral, and creative beings; in terms of our creation as a physical-spiritual unity in the image of God; and especially in terms of humankind's religious calling in life. Response to this calling is to be a whole response, not only with respect to the various areas of human life, but also with respect to the various functions of a person's nature.

Unless learning takes place, that is, unless curriculum brings the student to understanding, acceptance, and commitment, education will fail. For education to succeed, curriculum and pupil must be brought into vital contact so that genuine response takes place. One condition to such learning is that curriculum be well conceived, focused, organized, and directed. Another condition is that teaching be honored as a science; that is, that empirical studies in psychology and sociology be utilized so that due regard for the pupil's physical-spiritual wholeness may help ensure that the best procedures and methods in teaching are followed.

The most important condition to real learning is that the student be engaged, moved, and changed by the "word" of curriculum. Because such an encounter is in some ways as transcendent a happening as God's encounter of a person in Christian experience, the teacher's role is to do all in his or her power to keep vital curriculum and the unique individual in range of each other. Not concern for curriculum alone, nor concern for whole learning alone, but a persistent, watchful, creative joining of the two in vital teaching will characterize the wise teacher.

Any teacher worth her salt will believe and practice that what goes on in a classroom is nothing else than education *of* children, *for* children, and *by* children. The child, collectively and individually, is front and center, is the focus of it all, is the chief ongoing and ultimate concern of the teacher. What the child needs, what he/she ought to have, do, and become, is all-important. The *way* to do education of, for, and by children is through nothing else than subject matter—good, meaningful, disciplining, formative and interactive subject matter. By these always together, by artistic and scientific *closure* between the learner and the objective curriculum—only in this way does Christian education happen.

In heaven one day, when all of mankind's dichotomies, dualisms, and other follies are corrected, the monstrous divorce between the child and the curriculum will be ended—forever. The perpetual educational challenge to "come in further, come up higher," as Lewis puts it in *The Last Battle,* will be an invitation to educational closure. Educator and educand, encounter and response, subject matter and learning process will always be in range of each other, always engaging each other, always mutually enriching each other, and always in the service of the educational aims God has always had for humankind.

Major Educational Goals of Christian Schools

The major aims chosen at this level of educational philosophy should function midway, so to speak, between the school's over-arching goal (allegiance to Christ's kingdom, cultural obedience) and the teacher's specific lesson objectives (using a mathematical concept, stating the main point of a biblical parable). The school's major aims should be distinguished from but also function as a direct operational link between those broad goals having to do with human calling and those specific objectives having to do with pedagogical practices.

The school's major aims should also be distinguished from, though related to, all the goals it has in common with homes and churches. Along with them, a Christian school is concerned with the nurture of young persons' commitment to God in faith and obedience and to one another in loving relationships. Along with parents, the school, too, aims at their physical, social, and psychological development, and at their respect for and skills in the manual arts of shop, office, and kitchen. But in a division of responsibility these common aims are not primary in a school. They are collateral to what the school is mainly called to do by the Christian community that established it. Given that calling, the school's major aims should be those that fit directly with the formal, academic studies to which homes and churches cannot give their primary attention and to which the school may not fail to give its primary attention.

For anyone unseduced by the contemporary mania for the child's freedom, certainly for Christians, schooling is an *intentional* enterprise. The central child-benefit intention is that we adults hand down to the young, in the context of professionally taught academic studies—that is, with materials and in ways homes and churches and ordinary society are normally either not called to or are not competent in—our most cherished convictions and ways of living. For educational philosopher John Dewey this meant leading young persons to reflect on, to choose, and to live "the democratic life" in his contemporary society. For Plato this meant leading them to reflect on, to choose, and to live "the heavenly life" in his society. And surely for us this means leading young persons to reflect on, to choose, and to live the Christian life in our contemporary society.

Note those words: *reflect on, choose,* and *live.* These are the key aims or purposes for any serious school enterprise. To put it another way, let us call the aim of Christian education "Christian wisdom"—what is that wisdom? It is (a) insight, understanding, knowledge (b) directed for seeing moral options and making good commitments and choices, (c) culminating in good acts, expressive, existential acts. These are the goals that take fullest account of all that the Bible and all that science teach about the nature and needs of young persons.

I have used the terms *intellectual, moral,* and *creative* in writing about the kinds of growth the school should work at achieving. The point is not that these three describe persons completely, but rather that they encompass religious response; they are educational variants on the Heidelberg Catechism's emphasis on knowledge, righteousness, and holiness. In their inter-relationship these three are the biblical response of *knowing.*

Following, in summary fashion, are some important explanatory comments about the three major educational aims.

a) They are uniquely suited for religious growth appropriate to the school's competence and calling;

b) they are, in whole or in part, obviously more suited to some subjects or units or lessons than others, but are signals not to miss opportunities in any subject;

c) they do not imply parts or faculties in persons but rather express major functions of the wholeness and fullness of image-bearing that schools should address; nor are those aims really separable. They overlap, intertwine, are entailed in each other. But they are conceptually distinguishable;

d) they are intended to aid teachers directly in choosing text books, writing courses of study, planning daily objectives—and can help meet some of the frustration teachers feel in such planning;

e) they are equally applicable to both "separate-subjects" and "combined-subjects" approaches to curriculum, and to both radical transformationist and moderate transformationist views of Christian discipleship;

f) they are especially suitable to young persons' developmental and maturation needs; and,

g) to repeat, they are indispensable as linkage aims between the over-arching religious purpose of the school and the day to day objectives of the classroom teacher.

The Goal of Intellectual Growth

The increased momentum in Reformed circles toward praxis, sociology, and discipleship without a corresponding passion for theory, theology, and just plain intellectual rigor has propelled another bad disjunction, that between the intellectual goal and a new discipleship goal. Just as the earlier debate had to be lifted above the question whether we should teach children or subject matter, so this debate must be lifted above the equally fruitless question whether we should teach children for Christian discipleship or for intellectual/moral development through subject matter. As then, so now: the educational confusion and harm of either/or rhetoric needs to be exposed and rejected.

The new consciousness in Christian education wants to be singly and dramatically focused for servanthood, discipleship, obedience—meaning socially relevant. Such discipleship education must be firmed up and made more holistic with a rousing emphasis by its proponents on an old-fashioned education notion—the notion that intellectual discipline matters. Granted that in this area grievous sins have been committed by inflexible traditionalists. But is it even possible to have a Reformed school and not affirm clearly that it is first of all a reflective and thinking community? Can even transformationist discipleship be Christianly responsible without information, analysis, understanding, insight—thinking? Without such intellectual controls, discipleship would become a mindless activism, force-fed by teachers' slogans and indoctrination.

We ought to cringe every time we hear someone bad-mouth intellectual development. It is not the opposite of discipleship; discipleship is inconceivable without thinking. In all the writing on discipleship as knowing vs. doing, on decisional learning, or on responsibility theory, we find no separate emphasis on intellectual growth. Rarely, if ever, is it said that young persons must have insight, understanding, analysis. Instead in some of those writers intellectual learning is dismissed as "mind-stuffing," "pouring in facts," asking kids to "regurgitate" what teachers lecture at them. If teachers are guilty of such teaching we must object to it; surely we are past that in this enlightened age. But the corrective is not a grotesque anti-intellectualism, teaching in which students become discipled through pooled ignorance in "discussions," and go home ready to change the world through ignorance, passion, and cheap sloganeering. Let us hope that all educational leaders will affirm (and practice) that the first part of students' discipleship is to know what they are talking about—lest someone one day write a book about the closing of the Calvinist mind.

Typical discipleship advocates do not, I think, emphasize enough the celebration part of life in God's world. This shows in the way they most often handle subject matter; it gets to be mainly a vehicle for teaching about change and transformation. It all sounds so grim and austere, as if the school were mainly bent on indoctrinating little soldiers of the cross, spoiling good novels and poems and history and science with a geiger-counter mind-set bent on finding heresy and wickedness and darkness. Where is the celebration of the splendor of God's good earth and of the magnificent cultural inheritance of the ages? Where is the "music"—the excitement and reach and just plain joy of learning? Where is the rousing and eloquent case for subject matter—for the drama of history, the beauty of mathematics, the mysteries and wonders of science, the "food for the soul" of novels and poems, the knowledge and inspiration of religious studies?

Christ who is Lord over all owns all that is good and true and beautiful in the Father's world. According to the Reformed view of education, young persons must be taught to acknowledge this and to revel and work in the world in praise of Christ who redeemed it. For such celebration, good subject matter well taught is indispensable; it requires intellectual growth.

Reformed schools since the time of Calvin's Academy in Geneva have emphasized sturdy thinking and a rigorous curriculum—and produced some world-class tranformers. We should in our schools try to do no less today—to avoid cultural and religious illiteracy, to foster responsible transformers in our time, to celebrate the riches of our inheritance, and to pass on to the generations to come even more than we have received.

The Goal of Moral Growth

We diminish, stunt, and do educational aims a great disservice if we do not set moral education apart for special emphasis. If we say all of life is religion, and if that means related to God, then certainly it is also moral—moral being that part of life which is religiously decisional.

Christian liberals and secular humanists of many varieties have all through history sought to separate morality from its religious roots. In a final sense morality gets rooted in some religious perspective, of course, but operationally the separation can be made; its effects, when it is made, are melancholy at best.

When I speak of moral education in Christian schools, I want in no sense, operationally or in principle, to cut it loose from religion. Whatever I say about moral awareness, moral choice, and moral growth I mean to identify as nothing else than Christian religious awareness, Christian religious choice, and Christian religious growth.

Even so, to hold moral and religious as interchangeable would be a gross distortion. The word *religion* in education is broader than the moral. To put it another way, Christian education has other components. The word *religion* in Christian educational aims includes also, e.g., intellectual insight and understanding; it includes also creative participation and expression; so too eating and drinking, as the apostle Paul says, and planting trees and washing floors and keeping accounts and playing basketball. All of life, we say, if it is, as it must be, lived *coram dei,* before the face of God, is religious.

Further, by moral education I mean not at all moralistic education on the one hand nor mere decisional education on the other. Our goal must be not a Christian version of behavior modification (which smacks of pietism), nor a Christian version of values clarification, but the biblical version of covenant choice—which is piety through cultural obedience. Values-clarification is not enough; it is only site-preparation, only a species of the 'who am I' question; and includes too much of feelings and emotions. Decisional is not enough; it calls for action, but perhaps is only reaction. Merely changing behavior is low-order moral education. What is needed is *internalization* of commitment, choice, and values. To be Christian, behavior must be rooted in the other parts of the moral-religious chain. Before attitudes and behavior, before choices and commitments, must be emphasis on knowledge about, understanding of, insight into the complexities of any moral problem. Moral education means choice and commitment, with fear and trembling, because there are real crossroads, real options, not only between good and bad, but also between good and better. There are gray areas; therefore, before choice must be awareness and heightened sensitivity. New Testament discipleship means response to the love and law of Christ.

The goal of moral growth is a chief way the Christian school becomes a kingdom and covenantal adjunct of Christian homes and churches. For such growth, moral awareness and sensitivity are essential, especially the complexities of distinguishing right and wrong; for such growth, moral choices based on a religious commitment of the heart are essential. So, neither behavior-modification as a strategy nor moralism as a strategy is a good Christian school way of promoting Christian behaviors and attitudes. Values-inculcation needs superb pedagogy. It may not be mere indoctrination, mere imposition; it must be developmentally suited to the age and temperament of the child or adolescent. Inculcation must as much as possible allow for the learner's own inquiry and discovery. But underlying careful pedagogy is this reality, accepted by teacher and learner both: that some values are right and good and some are wrong and bad—and, most important, some become good or bad through misuse or circumstance or situation.

Moral education has not fared well in Christian schools. This is both regrettable and tragic. When one contemplates only casually the rich treasure for moral education at the surface or only just below the surface of much of a school's curriculum, one is struck with how the moral questions of right and wrong, good and bad, wicked and godly bristle out all over.

To foster moral development, schools need to uncover in the subject matter the tensions and issues presented by various world views in conflict—by what philosopher William Harry Jellema called *minds.* To him, minds meant more than intellectual systems. Minds meant outlooks, world views—and above all allegiances. We must find these minds in the subject matter. We must induct the young into the questions, the problems, before we try to give them the answers. We must make moral struggle a central goal of Christian education—what I call moral dissonance.

Teachers must prod students to see the moral complexities and ambiguities that abound in the student's experience and courses of study. Teachers must in fact, from time to time, introduce dissonance and moral sweating into the experience of young persons, to shake them loose from the easy answers or prejudices they prefer to moral complexities. Dissonance is a tool in promoting moral growth; as Jesus disturbed his listeners into new ways of thinking, so must we. In his parables he sought always to disturb, to make persons stop and think and search out answers. And the prophets said, Woe to those at ease in Zion.

It is a method teachers should practice. Why not let the disturbing questions run for a while, even adding to them? Why not foster a kind of holy dissonance, so that students struggle and sweat for a time as they themselves seek to apply Christian norms to the specific perplexing case, so that they come in this way to accept the problem as their own before the teacher offers answers. Such strategy, with the need to choose between alternative answers to internalized questions, would seem to be an important component of religious growth. It is difficult to know God's will; we must learn that the answer is not to quit searching but the opposite: to *sweat out* the matter and come to some choice and action. A great obstacle to doing (and at times to finding) the will of God is what Plato called appetite or desire and what St. Paul called our carnal nature. In neither case is desire wrong—rather desire is not itself the standard for action; desires must be understood and evaluated against a supernatural norm. It seems to me that if all of this is done carefully, pedagogically, Christianly, so as not to hurt the student, and is followed at the appropriate time with the teacher's telling and showing, we will foster covenantal commitment.

Anyone who believes and teaches others, especially children, that there really are no problems, that all questions are answered in our adult culture, or in our advanced modernity, or in the simplistic gospel of "letting Jesus come into your life," is a subversive person. We must teach that there is dissonance, that there always will be, maybe even in heaven; that issues and problems and mysteries and questions are blessings; that the essence of our imaging God is in the facing, surmounting, sweating, struggling, answering of questions and problems in the chain of seeing new questions and problems and struggling through them in an unending growth and sanctification. Of course, all of this must not only lead to worship, but be a process of worship. The essence of sin is denying the problems and living like an animal.

Hot-house Christianity is negative—true Christianity is positive and aggressive. Christians are often bored because they have not learned to live in the polar tensions of security and crisis. Security, yes—but not complacency, the Bible warns. James says, "The testing of your faith produces endurance." It will make you grow strong, help you learn to say "no," or "let me think," or "it depends." We must build such dissonance into young lives also.

137

Christian education is more concerned with immunization than with non-exposure. It will train toward freedom to choose the right from the wrong, rather than world-flight or unawareness of evil. The school's task is not conversion, but the implications of covenant, of kingdom membership. Decisions for Christ are not the *end* but the *beginning*—the beginning of a dangerous life, a life of crises, a life toward a Christian culture. We must root out a host of sub-Christian values and attitudes: provincialism, materialism, legalism, cynicism, and insecurity in this world. Only the best curriculum can really provide such child-centered education. The school's curriculum is the continuing material through which to help young Christians grow toward internal motivation and perfect liberty.

Modeling is also a catchword of education, and truly teachers (and all Christian adults) must be models for covenant living. But if the idea of modeling is left only personal, the Christian school is failing. The modeling must be in the education, in the history and literature and religion studies.

All of this is intentional in the school, but because God's will is a will of love and law, teachers must carry their derived authority in the signature of love and law. They must never violate a child's or adolescent's rights; they must respect the learning-teaching process. The kinds of problems posed and the amount of unsettling that a teacher does in order to reach the educational goals are questions of readiness and development, and will depend on the student's previous learning. Not insecurity is the goal of moral education, but free response to God and to the claims of his kingdom; the insecurities are subordinate to the higher goal of security in personal commitment to God.

As guides in such moral education, the following should be stressed:

1) As God's image bearers, young persons in a classroom are not objects but subjects; they are not to be manipulated by teachers but are to be educated as active responders. Whatever lower-order training as behavior modification they need because

of sin and perverseness must not be confused with the school's major aims.

2) Their response to the teacher's encounter of them with the school's subject matter is not by one or other of their "parts" but is a single response from within the religious unity of their persons.

3) That unitary religious response, whether of children or adults, the Bible prominently urges upon God's people in the covenantal words "knowing God in their hearts."

The Goal of Creative Growth

Children and adolescents are endowed with a marvelous creativity of heart and mind. Unlike adults who tend mainly to be conformists, young persons will live exuberantly between two worlds, their outward world with its pressures to conform to what others expect, and their interior world with its freedom to be the unique persons God created them to be. Surely, Christian teachers must honor that interior world. Alert to the fear and inertia that tend to invade that world, teachers must nurture the freedom of young persons to put their own signature on their own life. Along with the intellectual and moral growth of students, teachers must emphasize the young persons' *creative* growth.

Creative is perhaps not the best word, but I don't know a better one. I don't want just an action goal, but a psychological freedom and a commitment to become a responder, a participator—and then an actor, yes! Such creative growth is bigger than just going out and changing the world. Not just in the future but in their normal Christian development, young persons must be active participants in the learning process and in their unfolding ordinary life. They must rise above the lassitude or inertia or fear that characterizes the uncreative life. They must be brought to the freedom—on their level and according to their developmental stage—of Christian discipleship.

Stimulating creative growth includes stirring the juices of response and self-expression. This freedom begins in class: daring to ask questions, daring to suggest alternative answers, daring to be imaginative in science, daring to think aloud about what we could have done in this or that historical situation. More than just "gut responses," they should be responses after intellectual analyses and moral judgments have been made. Understanding and judging are not to be set over against but are an indispensable and continuous prelude to action, to discipleship. Refusing the easy way of merely reacting, of unknowingly or a-morally spinning off easy answers, the learner should get involved deeply in expressing solutions, freed for a productive contribution to life. Such personal growth and involvement are the end product of the curriculum and of the intellectual and moral growth good curriculum must promote.

Instead of merely lecturing and drilling students, the teacher must encourage them to discuss; instead of giving them pat answers to every social problem that the Christian faces, she must encourage them to think matters through; instead of asking them to color paper plates for their mothers in art classes, he must get them to express their feelings and ideas about the gospel and life with the media of the artist. In science the teacher must encourage them to compose experiments; in biblical studies she must get them to think through the message for themselves. In social studies, the Christian teacher must place a good deal of emphasis on the Christian approach to contemporary social issues. The student must be made to face the racial problem in Christian perspective, family relations in Christian perspective, and must be brought to ask about and to learn about a Christian view of work and recreation and private property and the welfare state. Throughout the curriculum the teacher must avoid merely acquainting the students with what has been thought and said and done by others, and get them to think and speak and act for themselves, as Christians. It is nothing but a pious wish and unwarranted hope that students trained to be passive and non-creative in school will suddenly, upon graduation, actively contribute to the formation of Christian culture.

Does the school's success with the creative growth of its pupils require special courses or can it be accomplished by a deliberate attempt to further such growth in the studies emphasized for intellectual and moral development? A Christian school should aim at creative growth in both ways. The implementing or methodological procedures must be aimed at active learning, inner learning, whole learning. This is more than a formal matter, more than a simple question of *how* this or that should be studied and taught. For example, much of the substance of a science course is altered when, say, the sixth grade teacher ceases to stress mastery of large blocks of scientific fact, in outlines on the board, or in daily assignments of three or four text-book pages, and adopts instead an experimental and discovery approach, through regular classroom demonstrations or in many and varied laboratory units. In both ways of teaching science, scientific data (facts, method, meanings, relationships) will provide the structure for movement and progress in the course, but the effects on the student will vary according to the method adopted. In the discovery way of doing things, the student stands a far better chance to get involved in active, inward, and whole learning, a kind of learning that can be transferable to open, experimental, creative participation in other areas of life—in playground disputes, at the family dinner table, in the give and take one day of adult inter-personal relationships in politics, daily work, or recreation.

Emphasis in historical, religious, literary, and many other studies, on facts and even meanings, aiming at highly important understandings (indispensable though these be to intellectual and moral growth) must be kept subordinate to a higher goal, namely, that of a growing freedom to *be* and to *act*. Students must be encouraged to come to their own questions, to ferret out meanings, above all to engage in free and open discussion in the classroom, with each other and with the teacher. When the teacher periodically strives for this (by planning, assignments, and general atmosphere) there will still be time and a better preparation for whole blocks of explanations and teaching by the text-book and teacher. Meanwhile, students will be growing by doing, growing toward self-acceptance and toward freedom from inaction, fear, and a passive way of life.

Once those learning goals we have designated "creative" are understood, it will also be understood that the whole focus of education must be what educators call an observable changed behavior. In a context of Christian educational aim, this expression may denote a student's whole involvement into life also viewed in its wholeness. Creative growth entails that the child or young person is understood as a complex human person, with private and public emotional, social, religious, intellectual, physical, moral, human needs. Creative growth means that the learners in their complexity and essential unity come to know themselves, to accept themselves, and, in the freedom gradually nourished within them, to express themselves, to commit themselves in the adventure of human living. They come, before the possibility and openness of life, as well as before its conventions, pressures, claims, and duties, to participate. They come to be involved, to do, to make, to produce, in short, to join those others around them in living a human life and in doing the world's work. They come to hear for themselves the call to be unique individuals, to live in community with fellow believers and with all persons, to be persons of faith, and withall, to accept their calling in life. Creative growth may produce outstanding artists, scientists, social workers, and craftsmen, but its success is far from depending on such outcomes,. The success of reaching this learning goal in the life of students should be measured by its effects in the great majority of students for ordinary human living. Success will depend on whether most students have opted for not a submissive, uncreative, nonparticipatory life but the opposite of this. The student's Christian life must come to be pointed outward, in human living, in living for cultural stewardship, in living the responding life of faith, in living within the Christian community, and in living within ordinary human society.

The Child in the Classroom

Our learning goals or aims depend squarely on the nature of the learner and on what we, as a result, judge his or her educational needs to be. Teachers, principals, and parents must understand and respect child-life and adolescent life—as the life of those of whom the Lord said, Let them come to me. Because they see each child as "child of God," a physical-spiritual unity, Christian teachers will be most diligent in their study of the child. They will make use of the data that the sciences of physiology, psychology, biology, and sociology supply for knowing what a child is like: for example, how fear, or hostility, or loneliness, or a deficiency in hearing or seeing affect learning; what variety of motivation, readiness, and learning styles there are; what are the effects on children of stable or disrupted homes, of good or poor nutrition, of racial harmony and discrimination, of emerging sexuality, and much more. A Christian view of the child requires that the empirical knowledge of the teaching-learning process be observed by the teacher as a matter of Christian professional conscience.

But more is needed. From the Bible, teachers learn about the physical/spiritual unity of young persons and about their endowments for life in God's world. In addition, to assess educational need we must do more than merely describe a learner, either empirically or revelationally; we must be normative as well. The nature and needs of the child are defined not only by empirically studying him, and not only with reference to his capacities as image of God, but especially by the fact of his religious calling. We learn from the Bible about what God's image-bearers ought to be and to do in the world.

Teachers should recognize that the proneness to sin is as real in children and adolescents as in adults, but also that God's claims and promises are equally real for them. Teachers must find their way with fear and trembling between that reality of sinfulness and that other reality of fragile sanctification, needing correction and firmness on the one hand and encouragement and freedom on the other. But the main job of schooling has to do with the implications of Christian life. Merely to provide nurture in prayer or piety or private morality is not enough. The common need of young persons to grow in the ability to fulfill their human/religious calling must be the continuing concern of the Christian school.

A Christian school must also all along the way give due attention to the individual differences and needs of young persons. In fact, one reason we should emphasize individual needs is to be more effective in helping each learner with the common needs. On the other hand, the clearer we get about those common needs, the freer we will be, psychologically and pedagogically, to experiment and innovate with individual needs. For then fences will be up: we will know both the extent and the limits of legitimate experimentations.

It is important that Christian schools provide good education for all normal young persons: for the slow learner and the fast learner, for the practically-minded and the theoretically-minded. A commitment to do this should be a prominent part of the school's general religious commitment, and the obligations it imposes should be religiously met.

But does not talk of good education, involving priority learnings and priority curriculum, imply the sort of aristocratic education from which reformers for some decades now have sought to liberate American education—an aristocratic education suited for only the brighter college-bound student?

A Christian school should, of course, reject any tendency to be only a college preparatory school, serving only, or mainly the academically minded; but it should also reject the charge that education organized around priority goals entails being such an elitist school. Rather, it should believe deeply that such education is precisely the sort of education *all* young persons need. The school should believe that such education is the best of all preparations for life, for the immediate life of young Christians as well as for their future life; it should especially believe that young persons for whom high school education will be terminal need such education. All children in the Kingdom are special—deserving of an elite education.

Precisely to avoid wrong-headed elitist or aristocratic education, the Christian school should resist the subversive way of meeting the needs of the slow learner and/or the practically-minded. That easy way is to substitute an education largely made up of all sorts of activity and practical subjects, as if such young persons were third class citizens in the Kingdom of God, somewhere below both the "philosopher-kings" and the "guardian" classes of society. The harder but more responsible way of meeting their needs requires that the school bend every effort to afford such persons the same high level education it gives to others.

The tendency of many contemporary schools, especially at the high school level, to give up on all but the top third or fourth of the class, for whom high college-board scores and acceptance by big-name colleges define educational aim, should be shunned by Christian schools. So should the notion that because some students do not move as fast as others, or have (often temporarily) different aptitudes and interests, they should on this account be fed educational bread and water from junior high school days on. This is rank injustice, a sort of educational wasteland. It is a by-product of the notion that a high school gets its identity chiefly as a college preparatory school instead of from what it really is, a place where not only college-bound students go for necessary maturative education but where also all other students must be given their last formal *school* preparation for understanding, choosing, and creatively living the Christian life.

Providing significant education for the slow learners, for the more practically-minded, for the unmotivated, for the late-bloomer is no doubt the hardest part of Christian education, but all students need the very best education a Christian school can offer. This is so because they must live thoughtfully, committedly, and creatively as Christian and as human in their future lives, whether they be carpenters, doctors, store clerks, parents, assembly-line workers, poets, or missionaries. Doubtless if more adequate measures were employed to meet the problem of these young persons, improved teaching would result all along the line for all students. But whatever structural and procedural methods are devised, the school should above all ensure that its major educational goals remain the ongoing, day-to-day goals also in these classes. For both the faster and the slower learners the right things must go on in the priority subjects.

The young persons in our classrooms are trying to adjust their independence and self-awareness to continued parental and community pressure. They resent this authority while they secretly need and look for it. Deep down they want to be not "of the world," but everything in them cries out for a place and a name and recognition in the world. They must be faced with God's will and calling for them and led to the point where they respond to that will. They must not merely react, mechanically or fearfully or obediently, but respond in an I-Thou commitment at the depths of life. They need the vital interaction of their faith with the surging reality of life around and within them. They need a school's curriculum materials to clarify that reality and to grow in their covenant life. For understanding and accepting the implications and risks of their calling, all young persons need Christian education.

Learning

A response at the depths of human consciousness was to be the human learning response to objective reality. It was an endowment of human nature that men and women, girls and boys, unlike evergreen trees and Hereford cow and Indian ponies and the Colorado river, were not only able but were in fact driven to be active and discriminating responders, moved and changed by their total environment. That environment included, as the reality behind all objective reality, God, in his law and love and in his presence at their right hand and left hand , whether they worked or played or worshiped. In that responding lay the possibility and the necessity of learning.

This learning must engage the whole person, and not merely her intellectual capacities. In those subjects that are able to foster significant moral growth, a mere intellectual mastery could block whole Christian growth. If a teacher teaches only about slavery, or only about the New Deal's response to the great depression, teaches only about starvation in India or history's religious wars, without deeply immersing young Christians in the great moral issues these subjects present, he is stopping short of Christian teaching. Further, a failure to reach the whole person results if subjects that can foster significant creative growth are so intellectualized or moralized that their creative potentials are ignored or run aground. This happens when, in the study of a poem or a painting or a novel, a teacher's obsession with its historical background, its moral tensions, its philosophical assumptions, or even its aesthetic theory, blocks its impact upon the learner as a work of art. Learning in a Christian school must be cumulative also with respect to the whole person, so that it becomes a response by the learner in all, not part of, his endowments and capacities.

Of course, not all children or adolescents are equally capable of extended intellectual learning, regardless of how competent a teacher is. In the case of some young persons, unrelieved pressures in that direction could snuff out other dreams, other passions, other attainments. The urge to practical involvements in life, to be a nurse, a farmer, or a heating expert, could be diverted or suppressed. The urge to creative activity, playing an instrument, writing poems, or making model airplanes, could be stifled or frustrated. Great harm could result if every child or adolescent were pushed, without relief, to continuous maximum intellectual performance. Such relief should be provided students within core studies but also in other sorts of curriculum areas, especially those that foster self-awareness and creative participation in school and in life. Although every young Christian must come to terms with the rational side of human life, and, on his level and according to his personality and ability, be educated for a rational participation in life, the school should adjust its pressures to the developmental stage of the child.

Of all its concerns that the right things do in fact go on in its priority subjects, a Christian school's concern for the learning *process* should be second to none. If intellectual, moral, and creative learnings are not to resemble more nearly their caricatures than real learnings, they must generate active learning. The student's growth must become a certain kind of awareness, a certain kind of involvement, such that learning response gradually becomes self-propelling. It must become self-propelling, moreover, in a way that is largely characterized by inquiry and by discovery. Within the conditions of good courses and good teaching, real learning comes as often through discovery as through disclosures. In a sense, since new material is personally appropriated and fitted existentially into a pattern of previous learnings, true learning is always discovery. When a child finally comes to pray his own prayer, thus appropriating what was taught, he may be said to have discovered God. But even in the more functional sense of exploring, of discovery, cognitively and perceptually, much of real learning is uncovered by young persons themselves. Thus in science studies especially the methods of inquiry and discovery must be stressed, but in many other subjects as well. Such discovery, intellectually or morally, not only fastens down what is learned; it is generative of new inquiries and new discoveries. In this way the student learns to learn.

Life is not long enough, of course, for young persons to discover in this exploratory sense all that they should learn; they need to be told, to be shown, to be taught many things. They must be led and guided into progressively more remote studies, in mathematical relationships, say, or in comparative literature, or Christian doctrine. But if in the process they do not periodically get caught up with the magic and wonder of discovery, with the challenge of searching things out for themselves, with the rewards of struggling through the complexity and difficulty of a problem into the light of understanding, there may be intellectual accretion but not growth. When subjects, even the best subjects, produce only accretions and not growth, they are not generative, and the learnings they stimulate are not vital learnings. Such learning does not contribute to Christian growth.

If a Christian school faculty believes that a child is defined not only by describing him but also by his calling in the world, if they further believe that this calling requires above all that the learner be a responder to God and to life under God, and therefore also to his schooling; and if that response is to be modeled after the biblical idea of knowing in its three dimensions, then that faculty has a solid religious basis for one of the most important applications it must make, namely, choosing the major learning goals it will emphasize in the school.

Traditional or Progressive?

In a Christian school, the students' educational growth by means of curriculum is at every point challenged to be a response to God's encounter of them in nature, in culture, in history, and in the common occurrences of daily life. That is the educational application of the big religious vision.

But are we convinced that Christian schools (Calvinist, Catholic, Lutheran, and all the rest) ought to be rooted in, embody in their programs, and then articulate to the young Christians in them, a comprehensive religious vision for all of life, all the time? Or shall we be content with considerably less: with merely creedal and ceremonial religion, with body and soul dichotomies, this-worldliness and otherworldliness? Shall we walk afraid, heads down, alienated, mere protesters, living in a way-station next to the main streets of North America? Shall our schools be a historically authentic, culturally relevant, religiously vital alternative to contemporary public schooling or private little ghettos for good basic education (maybe) plus some rudimentary spiritual nurture that homes and churches should really be providing?

Or, uneasy before these choices, are we headed down another road, almost in relief? Are we re-doubling our efforts to be *avant-garde*, and relevant, and really modern, by grasping almost frantically for each new innovation that contemporary technocrats in education can dream up? These innovations may or may not be as good as claimed; the point is that they are no substitute for foundational thinking about Christian schooling. In fact, innovations can be diversionary from the real questions in an almost subversive way. Thus, being busy with technology, with procedures and *how* questions, we don't ask about the nature and needs of young persons theologically and empirically. We buy into secular thinking about behavior modification, affective education, endlessly changing report cards, the open classroom, mini courses, and always relevancy—in one or another form of the tired life-adjustment slogans of defunct progressivism. So too with Christian text-books, course of study writing, work-shops—we turn to these activities in almost audible relief from first-order questions about the school's religious vision, its priority learning goals, and its priority curriculum commitments.

Neither is it enough to talk about Bible study and devotional periods, or about Christian, caring teachers, or about controlling the sex-and-drugs scene. It is not enough even to talk about "discipleship" and "living the Christian life in contemporary society"—fundamentalist schools say the same things. We must talk about the big religious vision. That vision finds values in the past and in the present.

It is a lonely journey to walk between the crowds that have separated on the issue of traditional vs. progressive education. The slogans don't help but hinder; the winner/loser exhilaration is spent; and the "simple" answers are horribly complex. It may be that progress lies down the road of only the best of both the old and the new education, the tested vitalities of both. And that won't be surprising, given the momentum of history. For while history has its demonic momentum as well, those who are open to history's real gift to moral creative persons will find that the new moments in the human search bring better insights and progress. Our religious vision asks for an honest equilibrium between the best of traditional and the best of modern education. In Christian schools, our traditions and our openness will be our guide to proper wholeness in goals, curriculum, and methods.

CHAPTER THIRTEEN

Then Gladly,
Madly Teach

*Education never takes place without passion and
commitment—as indeed all good teachers have always
known; as all who have had such teachers know.*

There are at least two kinds of requirements you should meet in
order to become a good Christian school teacher. The first one is
educational competence. This does not necessarily mean you
must be an "A" student. It does mean that you should possess the
instincts, the habits, and the preparation of a *student,* that is, of one
who has mastered the basic skills and data of learning and has to
some extent been formed by its disciplines. You also must intend
to continue being a student for as long as you teach, so that your
pupils may be inspired by the adventure of learning, just as you
are.

But it is a second set of requirements—four essential qualities
of mind and heart—that I wish to discuss here in more detail.

The Religious Heart

The Christian schoolteacher does well, I think, to remember often
that his or her task is one of total religious education. By this I do
not mean missionary zeal, or instruction in piety, or the teaching
of church doctrine (although no Christian teacher will be indifferent to opportunities at any of these points). I mean rather the nurture of pupils and students at the religious center of life, at that
point where the inner person meets the outer world of habits, of
commitments, and of conduct. I have in mind this: that Christian

education is both an embodiment of and an agent to what may be called a Christian culture; and *second*, that, because the first is true, the Christian teacher finds in this fact his chief reason for being. If there is a difference between Christian school teaching and public school teaching, the difference must be found here, or all other differences become unimportant or meaningless.

It is still useful, I think, to say that a Christian schoolteacher *stands for* the parents in the matter of Christian education. I take it that parents have the assignment in the first place to nurture their children in a total way of life, of Christian life. Such total education goes beyond the calling and competence of the church; it is the parents' responsibility to provide it. And insofar as this is beyond the competence of the parents, they call upon the teacher to do it for them.

You as a Christian teacher will then be a religious force in the life of your students—by example, no doubt, but particularly by the kind of education you offer. A chief part of this education will be the uncovering of Christian insights and principles through the agency of books and the subjects studied. Apart now from the indispensable subjects that provide skills and tools, it is the "content" subjects that are the means to such education. You will remember that education is "leading toward answers," but only after the real questions have been asked, and only after students have come to understand the questions. Only then can types of answers be distinguished: Christian, anti-Christian, non-Christian, sub-Christian. It is such probing into truth, by means of analytical thinking and judgment (at the proper learning-level, of course) that will help form the students at the religious center of their lives.

Such education will achieve this not in a vacuum but in a truly educational sense, that is, at the frontiers of the student's own rational-moral awakening, in contact with life in its most real sense. Contrary to some proponents of practical learning, this encounter will not be less real because it comes via books and ideas but will for that very reason be the more dramatic and significant. It will be coming to the student through the open doors of his or her mind and imagination. For a child or adolescent, powerful ideas, universal qualities, and living options can be more real than the tumultuous diversities of "experiences."

All of this needs the expert tutelage of a teacher who has the necessary "maps" to the terrain—but also a passion for the religious heart. Given these, all of life can be shown to be religious, not in terms of our easy distinctions between sacred and secular (as, e.g., with respect to songs), certainly not in a sectarian sense, but *educationally,* in the way Joshua's words may be extended for our day: "Choose ye this day whom ye will serve."

This challenge must be uncovered in many places in the curriculum, and always the student must be made to see three things: *first,* that the challenge is present in this or that form; *second,* how he is tempted to dodge it in this or that manner; *third,* how Christian response lies in seeing the real challenge and in meeting it.

Such nurture in terms of ideas and life in religious tension will thus not be an imported moralism or intellectualism *next to* the study of the Bible, history, literature and the arts, or science. Rather, it will *rise up out of* these subjects and will involve the student at that point where she is image-bearer. This is what we mean by rational-moral education. It aims at the unity of knowledge and experience ultimately in God, and the commitment of mind and heart and life ultimately to God. That is to say, the chief end of the pupil, too, is to know God and to enjoy Him forever.

Something like this constitutes the chief responsibility of the teacher. To bring it off is almost impossible. Yet it needs trying through passionate, unflagging effort. This objective is really the only justification there is for Christian schools. If it is to be done, your faculties will have to work at the course and unit objectives in keeping with this over-arching goal, and you will have to see yourself as the indispensable link in the whole process. To succeed, you will need a firm and settled faith, but also a restless spirit in search of new insights into the meaning and relevance of the faith—educationally. For this you will need the religious heart of the teacher.

The Enthusiastic Thrust

As in rocketry, so in teaching: thrust is crucial. To be a good teacher, you will need a good deal of thrust, for which the solid fuel is enthusiasm. This combination is particularly effective because it is self-replenishing: enthusiasm breeds enthusiasm, in yourself and in your students.

The word *enthusiasm* comes from two Greek words meaning "in" and "God." It therefore suggests the idea of being God-possessed. A teacher's enthusiasm may, then, flow right out of the religious heart, perhaps in a kind of Pentecost—something the teaching profession needs most of all.

But take the word in its more general and common sense. It then means at least that its possessor is a positive, buoyant spirit, one who believes in what she is doing, who gets excited about it, who is therefore convincing, motivating, inspiring. It is the opposite of defeatism, cynicism, detached arrogance or self-centeredness.

In some cases an enthusiast may generate more heat than light, or may be such an activist or utopian that he drives his colleagues farther into their shells; in such cases, he is best ignored.

Enthusiasm in the good sense, however, is indispensable to the teacher. We have all endured teachers who lacked it. At best they were matter-of-fact and dull, certainly they did nothing for us; at worst they made God's gift of subject matter a burden and perhaps made us cynical about the teaching profession.

We recognized the good ones, too, of course. The difference was not that good teachers never got angry, or were always cheerful, or never dull, or always gave meaningful assignments, and always got tests back on time. They had many things to learn and to improve. But there was one thing they had: belief in what they were doing. The good teacher taught, most of the time, with excitement, with a light in his eye. The very situation, you there in your seats, and he up there in front, was bigger than its parts. History for him was high adventure, and you knew it. When he taught poetry, how it was made and what it did, or when she digressed on music or architecture, you and your friends were caught up in it.

When she heckled you on writing neatly or spelling correctly, or when he talked to you about thinking honestly or about self-confidence and self-criticism, or about growing up inside with the true and the good and the beautiful—then the light broke through and you saw what he meant and you went over to his side. The moment didn't always last, but a glimmer stayed on in a corner of your mind and one day it came back to you and was yours for real.

If you want to teach, believe in it the way a salesperson seems to believe in the product—and you will likely strike sparks off the minds of those who sit before you. A teacher can't be good at it without enthusiasm.

The Humorous Control

When life in a classroom runs off into chaos because of creeping disorder or paralyzing disinterest, you need a sense of humor. You really needed it before the situation deteriorated, for perhaps half of the bad situations that develop in a classroom are the fault of the teacher, his lack of humor, that is. And, of course, amidst the ruin of a bad situation you need it all the more.

By humor I don't mean telling funny stories, although this is an art worth developing. I have in mind rather a *sense* of humor—an attitude toward self, other persons, and the whole human situation. It is a perspective out of which to view the world, the flesh, and the devil. It is a principle of unity that holds together the comic diversities of life and sets you with composure and serenity above the tensions of duty and justice and "the principle of the thing."

You might say that humor is compounded of compassion, intelligence, and humility. Humor enables you to step back and say to yourself, "take it easy." It keeps you from ever looking into a mirror, figuratively or literally, without breaking out in a gentle smile—at yourself. It enables you to see others as they see themselves and to see yourself as others see you. Humor keeps you from taking yourself too seriously and helps you to take others more seriously. It protects you from that intensity which can easily be confused with competence, but also from that laziness which can be confused with relaxation. And a sense of humor cannot live in the same house with pretense and phoniness.

Humor keeps you mellow, pliable, able to roll with life. It will not lower standards, obstruct justice, or hide the truth. But it will season justice with mercy, logic with understanding, indignation with compassion. A sense of humor helps a person to know himself, and therefore to know that for human beings, who are not God, there is never the final system that is not subject to improvement—by someone else.

Humor may then keep the enthusiastic thrust and the religious heart under control, rooted in reality. Its very nature is to expose fanaticism, provincialism, and all the easy notions of world betterment. It will keep the custodians of orthodoxy from bitter militarism, the exponent of religious respectability from pharisaism, the defenders of law and morality from legalism and witch-hunting. It will also keep the pious from self-righteousness and the virtuous from prudery.

Humor comes up out of the depths of a person. Its steady vision has a way of cutting through the shells and shams that separate people. It can settle the turbulence of the spirit and restore a person to self and to others. It discovers and matures the common humanity that unites us, and keeps us in communion with each other, particularly when disagreements tend to alienate us. And finally, because self-knowledge and self-criticism are the first parts of true religion, I dare say a sense of humor will help us also in our relationship with God. Humor in this sense, as both an outlook and a way of life, can help bring about and maintain a kind of composure without which life would be cold and brittle and hollow.

As a teacher you need the humorous control as a check-point in interpersonal relations. When things fall apart in a classroom there will be a common base of sympathy and mutual acceptance on which to rebuild, without the undue anguish of hostility or the struggles of saving face. You will get on better with parents even though they are notoriously unhumorous about their children's rights and virtues. Living with your principal will be easier, too, when she gives you more paper work, more committee work, more supervision—too much external stuff, you say, not the heart of the matter.

Above all, you need a sense of humor for survival with your fellow teachers. For always there are some, one or two or three, who bother you. You either imagine it, or it is true, that they are stuffed shirts, not growing but merely swelling in their job. Perhaps you think they criticize you behind your back. They seem hypnotized by their own virtues. You are sure they are out to pasture, smug and secure: they have their job, a fairly decent income, long vacations, routines all set. These things or others bother you. Then you need a sense of humor to help you discover that you're all wrong about them, or to help you live with the fact that you're terribly right about them.

And you need a sense of humor all day long: in study halls, in playground supervision, with those slow learners, with those bright ones who are so slow of heart to understand and accept your priceless offerings. And of course you need it all the time just to live with yourself. Pray for it, work for it—the humorous control.

The Bold Spirit

If humor thus controls your enthusiasm, and these two give shape and force to your religious vision, you are on the way to becoming equipped for the bold life of the teacher. For the teacher must above all be of valiant spirit. Teachers should, I believe, be in trouble more than they are, for trouble would seem necessarily to be an occupational hazard of the profession. The teacher speaks to his students, but through them (as well as in speeches and written articles) to their parents and their communities.

That this is not always so goes against the whole sense of the profession. In particular, Christian teachers will offer this involvement as a service and feel required to give it as an obligation. For they stand in the prophetic tradition, having both the message and competence for the job. Also, of course, the community desperately needs their insights, conscience, wisdom, and their leading.

If this happens, if there is a good contact between teacher and community, there may well be what I have called trouble. There will occasionally be the rattle of small-arms fire, and even now and then the shock of mid-sized explosions. And this, I believe, will be not bad but good. For if tensions and disagreements develop, it will mean that the teacher is working at her calling. That is to say, the teacher's calling requires that she live at the frontiers where the battles of the spirit are joined. Whether in economics, art, literature, history, or Christian doctrine, there exist opposing views, values, and practices. Not always, of course, nor on all levels in equal intensity. But when opposed views are present they must be dealt with.

The teacher is both equipped and called to lead the way here—in the classroom and wherever else he has good occasion to speak. He does this by exposing and challenging alien and secular loyalties and by pointing out the more excellent way. He does this with books, often through a study of the past, and always educationally rather than dogmatically, aiming at understanding and commitment rather than mere verbalization. And it must be done in elementary school as well as in college, in the community as well as in the school.

The Christian teacher will be concerned with the moral and religious tensions of life, as these lie at the heart of any society in any period of history. With her insights and books and the curriculum itself, the teacher will expose the real sickness of human systems and the human heart, while at the same time pointing up the good and the true and the beautiful that the human spirit, through God's grace, has brought about. This means that evidence of sickness in the hearts of the students as well as in the Christian community must also be addressed.

Education has to do with such diagnosis and with the cures that come through Christian insight and commitment. The teacher makes judgments in terms of the history and wisdom of the ages, that is, in the context of books and curriculum, always under the light and discipline of Scripture. Teachers must, of course, be pedagogically wise and remain positive, careful not to hurt students or antagonize the community. The teacher must not be arrogant, reckless, concerned with winning arguments. The aim must be persuasion, conversion.

Even so, the bold teacher will meet opposition. Probing and diagnosing and prescribing is bound to unsettle students. This will happen, for example, when she makes war upon prejudice or provincialism, on ignorance or materialism. The bricks of a Christian school or the creeds of faith do not keep these evils away from us. Thus the teacher, by means of books and curriculum and articles and speeches, engages these evils and teaches students to engage them. Prejudice must be exposed and replaced by insight and judgment, compassion and conviction; provincialism with its arrogance and truncated solutions must make way for the perspective and humility that come with the larger vision; the materialism of suburban religious America no less than that of doctrinaire communism or exploitive capitalism must be challenged and replaced by the claims and illumination of the Spirit; and the cozy and comfortable ignorance which breeds the foregoing must be replaced with the restless search for knowledge, understanding, and wisdom.

This is the kind of Christian liberal education and the examined life that you are called into. If you work at these and related objectives you will become the leader you are called to be. But you will need the bold spirit to bring it off. You will not always be trying to figure out the climate but will help make the climate. You will not merely dance to a tune, but will help to call the tune. You will not forever be walking with your ear to the ground, but rather with your head up, where it should be.

Even though this bold spirit may be hazardous and get you into trouble, you will know that anything less is not good enough. You will know that the teacher who does not at times set loose the cross-winds of debate, whose ideas do not on occasion stir up strong loyalties on the one hand or indignant opposition on the other, is probably the teacher who hasn't yet finished his apprenticeship. Certainly, the one whose teaching arouses little or no reaction at all seems to lack integrity. There is a lesson here, I think, in the fate of Socrates and in a deeper sense, in the experience of our Lord Himself.

To be a teacher in this sense needs tact and wisdom. It needs the religious heart, the enthusiastic thrust, and especially the humorous control. But most of all, it needs the bold spirit. The teacher who has these could rise in the community's esteem above the level of the banker, the doctor, or the successful car salesman. The rise may be slow, even painful, and the teacher will have to earn it, for as things stand, the burden of proof is on her. If the elevation does come, it will come because the teacher is recognized as the spokesperson for learning in the community.

As such, your chief work will be in the classroom, shaping and molding, by God's grace, the minds and hearts of children and young people. But a part of your task inevitably will also be to speak to the community wherever you and the community meet. If you are wise and utilize generously the fourfold qualities of mind and heart set forth above, you will be better equipped to stand resolute and competent at that point of meeting. Then, as time passes, chances are that the community, and certainly your students, will come more and more to hear you out. Your scholarship will help here, of course, but those other qualities of heart and mind will have suitably focused your scholarship for educating the young in your care. Then you may well find that the teaching profession is becoming for you the high adventure you once thought it could be.

CHAPTER FOURTEEN

A Few Concluding Words

I will walk in the presence of the Lord
in the land of the living.
Ps.116.9

I believe the Christian day school will be judged to be necessary only to the extent that Christianity is judged to be full-orbed and all-embracing, including all of life, all the time. The starting point for such Christianity is that religion must be seen in the perspective of both creation and redemption.

Christian schooling is many things—buildings, buses, finance, curriculum, and more. But we must remember that it in principle has a two-fold task: restoring persons to a pre-fall "completeness" and directing such restored persons in the way God originally commanded them to go. His three commands given in the beginning were really a single command. Piety, community, and culture were together to promote *shalom*, to promote the love, peace, joy, and kindness which Paul later calls the fruit of the Spirit. Piety, community, and culture together were to lead to that fulness of life of which the garden tree, the Tree of Life, was the sacramental sign and seal.

Christian schooling is most stunningly students growing into this fulness of life, under the impact of this education. It is students developing responsible insight into life—the life of the human race through history and literature, the life of God's world through science, the laws of God's world through mathematics. It is the human personality developing appreciations for other people while at the same time coming to conscious understanding of the real nature of their difference from other people. Christian education is developing compassion with humility and self-respect, and developing appreciation for the intangibles of virtue and courage and duty and tolerance and beauty. It is the development of competence but no less of conscience. It is training in know-how but never at the expense of know-what or why. Christian education is not only a mastery of means but especially always a mastery of the ends and of values.

Through this kind of Christian education, the students recognize God as the source and fulfillment of all meaning and truth, and give themselves in a quest for meaning and truth through study, insight, and contemplation. The students see God also as the source and fulfillment of all justice and love, and give themselves in a quest for these through discernment, commitment, and act. And the students know God also as the source and fulfillment of all freedom and creativity, and give themselves in a quest for new creations and for personal freedom in work, in stewardship, and in self-expression. Thus the students will grow in knowledge of God who first knows persons in their endowments and wholeness. Such mutual knowing is the essence of covenant relationship. Applying that religious perspective to education ensures that the students' deepest needs are met.

Christian schooling is like the stable in C. S. Lewis' Narnia story. The stable was old, cramped, even mucky. Schooling too may seem dull, commonplace, and a burden. But when you entered the stable, all was different—an open vista, gold with Aslan's glory—and a voice said: Come in further, come up higher. Education in Christian schools can be like that, can make sons and daughters of God complete, can bring them to glory—in further, up higher. *Let children come.*

A Last Story

Jesus told the story of the son who squandered his inheritance. When he came home, he thought he should live backstairs as a servant. He came home to avoid responsibility, to avoid the problems of the world.

To us, as to him, Jesus says: Here—a robe, a ring, shoes; here, a party and a fatted calf. For you were lost and are found, were dead and are alive. Here, not a survival or subsistence life, but in the family quarters. Take on the responsibilities of sonship. Here once again you are daughters and sons, back in your father's house.

We are home—back in our Father's house, our Father's world, living in covenant with him. That is our reasonable religion. Hallow the earth, garden, sheep, number work like math, word work like poems and history, art work and science—all of it is religion, hallelujah. Recover the vision; make it vital and productive in our day—and in our children's lives.

Let's celebrate!

A Statement of Principles

Note: This statement was formulated by Dr. Beversluis as a model for use by Christian school societies.

The basis of this union is the Bible accepted as God's inspired and infallible revelation by which he directs us in our faith and life. On this basis we hold the following as religious principles for Christian education.

1. **Creeds**: that the Reformed creedal standards set forth truly the Bible's teaching about God and humanity's relation to God in creation, in the fall, and in salvation through Jesus Christ.

2. **Calling**: that the Christian faith entails not only creedal commitment but also religious obedience in a comprehensive life orientation within a world and life view.

3. **Christ in Culture**: that although in the fallen state human sin and guilt radically alienate us from God, darken our minds, and misdirect human life and culture, salvation and renewal through Christ radically restore us as image of God and reaffirm our calling to cultural obedience; and, further, that such obedience described in Genesis as dressing the garden, subduing the earth, and having stewardship over all things (and now including all extensions of that mandate in contemporary life and culture) must, together with obedience to the gospel mandate, be understood as obedience to Christ and therefore as an obligation of Christian sanctification.

4. **Schools and the Christian Life**: that when parents seek help in rearing their children for obedience of such range and scope, they should seek such help not in schools that by public law are forbidden to give it, but in schools which by their very existence are required to give it; and, further, that Christian teachers, who have their own call-

ing as teachers, thus become coworkers with parents in promoting within young persons an understanding of, a commitment to, and a creative participation in the Christian life within contemporary society.

5. **Image of God and the Learner**: that as image of God, young persons in the schools must be understood 1) in their personal wholeness—physical, spiritual, social, psychological; 2) as persons existing in a religious relationship to God in which work and worship though extrinsically distinguishable are nevertheless inseparable; 3) as persons uniquely assigned a cultural-religious task in the world; and 4) as persons whose endowments for intellectual understanding and insight, for moral awareness and choice, and for creative expression and participation uniquely equip them for their task.

6. **Learning Goals and Curriculum**: that given the foregoing, the schools are obligated as *schools*, and appropriate to the great range of learning levels and readiness within young persons, to give major attention to the young persons intellectual, moral, and creative endowments, so that in true knowledge, righteousness, and holiness young persons may progressively come to accept their calling as prophets, priests, and kings in their daily life; and, further, that given this calling and these learning goals, the schools are obligated as *schools*, and appropriate to the great range of learning levels and readiness in young persons, to organize a curriculum that most suitably encounters young persons with the range and scope of human religious life in all of its natural, social, historical, and cultural conditions.

7. **Christian Schools and Christian Community**: finally, that because Christian education based on these biblical principles will serve the common good, not only of public life but especially of Christian communal life, it is the obligation of the whole Christian community, and not just parents of children in the schools, to pray for, to work for, and to give generously in the support of Christian schools; and that this, too, is an obligation of Christian sanctification and obedience to Christ.

Sources

Chapters

The First Story, Chapters One, Two, Three, Five, Six, Seven, Eight, Twelve, Fourteen, and The Last Story: manuscripts for articles and speeches, class lecture notes, and many miscellaneous notes, from the 1950s to 1990s; plus short bits from published materials.

Chapter Four: chapters II and III of *A Biblical Approach to Philosophy of Education*, condensed.

Chapter Nine: a manuscript from the 1970s.

Chapter Ten: excerpts from Chapter IV of *A Biblical Approach to Philosophy of Education.*

Chapter Eleven: chapter 3 of *Christian Philosophy of Education.* (Used with permission.)

Chapter Thirteen: article from *The Reformed Journal*, September 1960. (Used with permission.)

Epigraphs

Chapters One, Two, Six, Eleven, and Thirteen: various manuscripts and notes.

Chapter Three: Calvin College Chapel talk.

Chapters Four (first epigraph) and Seven: A Biblical Approach to Philosophy of Education.

Chapters Four (second epigraph), Eight, and Fourteen: the Bible.

Chapters Five, Ten, and Twelve: various speeches.

Chapter Nine: "The Covenant and Education," *The Reformed Journal*, November 1953.

N. H. Beversluis
Bibliography

Entries are listed chronologically within divisions.

Books and booklet

A Biblical Approach to Educational Philosophy for the Christian Reformed Church. Doctoral Thesis for Columbia University, 1966. 390 pages. Ann Arbor, Michigan: University Microfilms, Inc.

Christian Philosophy of Education. 79 pages. National Union of Christian Schools, Grand Rapids, Michigan, 1971.

Toward a Theology of Education. 32 pages. Calvin College Occasional Papers, Vol. 1, No. 1, Grand Rapids, Michigan, February, 1981. Also on-line in "Classic Writings in Reformed Christian Education," Calvin College Education Dept., at: www.calvin.edu/%Erkeeley/monoweb/main.htm.

Articles, Reviews, and Reports

"Christian Education in the Classroom," *The Envoy,* February 10, 1950, p.4.

"The Covenant and Education," *The Reformed Journal,* November 1953, pp. 3-7.

"Bible Teaching in the Schools," *The Reformed Journal,* July/August 1954, pp. 13-15.

"Toward a Christian Culture," *Consolidation News,* Eastern Christian School Association, Fall, 1954; *Reformed Journal,* February, 1955, pp. 15-16.

"The Life in God," *Centennial Messages,* pp. 6-12, Back to God Hour, Chicago, Ill., 1957.

"Then Gladly, Madly Teach," *The Reformed Journal,* September, 1960, pp. 5-8.

"The Composition Gap," *Christian Educators Journal,* V. I No. 1, Fall 1961, pp. 12-15.

"Toward a Philosophy of Christian Education," *The Reformed Journal,* October 1962, pp. 15-18; November 1962, pp. 6-9; and January 1963, pp. 23-27.

"First Order Issues in Christian Philosophy of Education," *Christian Educators Journal*, V. 10, April 1971, pp. 15-19. Also on-line in "Classic Writings in Reformed Christian Education," Calvin College Education Dept., www.calvin.edu/%Erkeeley/monoweb/main.htm

"Educational Reform or Demolition," *The Banner*, August 31, 1973, pp. 8-10; review of John Holt, *Freedom & Beyond.*

"Meeting the Common Need,*"* *Christian Home and School*, July/August, 1980, pp. 6-7.

"The Future of Christian Education," *The Banner*, July 20, 1981, pp. 14-16.

In Their Father's House; A Handbook of Christian Educational Philosophy. 30 mimeographed pages. Prepared for Christian Schools International (CSI), March 1982.

"What's a College For? A Review Essay," *The Banner*, August 27, 1984, pp. 14-15; review of Theodore Plantinga, *Rationale for a Christian College.*

"Building the City Upon a Hill," *The Reformed Journal*, September, 1986, pp. 19-22; review of James Bratt, *Dutch Calvinism in Modern America.*

"Parents, Preachers, and Christian Schools," *The Banner*, January 2, 1989, pp. 18-20.

"The Christian Story and the Christian School," *Christian Educators Journal,* October 1994, pp. 31-33; review of John Bolt, *The Christian Story and the Christian School.*

"The Two Sides of Christian Education and Major Learning Goals in Christian Education," (Chapters 3 and 4 from *Christian Philosophy of Education*), in *Voices From the Past: Reformed Educators*, Donald Oppewal, Ed., University Press of America, 1997, pp. 122-154.